AF488398

A Visible God

An anthology

Edited by
Rev. Erin GH Beardemphl

A Visible God

An anthology

ELYSSAR PRESS

Printed in the United States of America

First Printing, 2022
ISBN 979-8-9853686-2-8

Elyssar Press
175 Bellevue Ave
Redlands, CA 92373

www.ElyssarPress.com

Cover Photo by Jessica Lea
Cover design by Stephanie Aoun Bou Karam
Book design and production by Stephanie Aoun Bou Karam
Editing by Samar Hage

Library of Congress Cataloging-in-Publication Data
Catalogued as: biblical;psalms;artistic interpretation;personal interpretation;multimedia;meditation;photography;tie-dye;fiber art;
quilt collage;watercolor

Table of Contents

A note from the editor

There have certainly been a number of books written to honor and explore the Psalms. Some have a decidedly academic bent, some aim to set the Psalms to tunes yet unheard. There have also been a number of picture books created, from colorful children's illustrations to artistic coffee table tomes. There is a temptation to simply flip through these pages, glimpsing the images quickly and then move on.

Our aim was to create a picture book that honors the psalms in a new way, a book which shares with others our experience of the Divine; a picture book that you could simply flip through, but with which I suggest you take your time.

Consider starting with an image, examining it and asking yourself: What do I notice first? What catches my attention the most? Next, read through the corresponding psalm, and identify words and phrases that stand out to you. Then, ponder the artist's descriptive explanation. Consider the words of the psalm alongside the interpretation or process of the artist: What stays with you? Do the artist's words bring surprise? assurance? discomfort? Finally, reach again for that image: What do you now notice? What new perceptions have you gained? Continue your meditation for as long as the image inspires you to do so. Take in one image at a time, for there is no rush. Stay with it, and consider its depth. You might even find yourself approaching one image more than once.

Our idea, you see, was to make a book that allows the reader to slow down, and to experience these ancient writings from an unusual perspective. There are many ways to reflect on what you've seen: quiet stillness, journaling, creating your own images...but start here. And take your time.

Introduction

It's an easily made mistake to think of the Psalms as a "book," for most of the time we encounter them either in reading or as spoken, complete with chapters and verses. They're found in the middle of the Bible (aka the "Big book"), alongside other diverse writings, so we often locate them among the literary genres such as histories, legal works, teachings, satires, prophecies, letters and even gospels.

While they work well that way too, it's always helpful to remember that the Psalms were a hymnbook for the people of God, the Jews, who used these songs to give voice to their life circumstances in relationship with that God. With 150 opportunities, a wide range of experiences come to the fore, both similar and unique. And they can be wonderfully personal. Though there is a power to common experience, be it in worship or in a concert hall (or a roadhouse), we all hear the music differently. From the wild hope of Psalm 91 (God as "refuge") to the brutality of Psalm 137 (v.9 "Happy shall they be who take your little ones and dash them against the rock!"), there may be something for everyone, something for anything.

This also applies to the expressions. Even in modern times, the best musicians who use words are character- ized by a diverse "catalog." Take for example Aretha Franklin – from the play and pointedness of "Respect" to the sheer grandeur of her best takes on "Amazing Grace," or the Beatles – the giddy hopefulness in "I Want to Hold Your Hand" to the pathos of "Eleanor Rigby." Great musical art emerges from real life's varieties, then transcends them, only to return us to terra firma, perhaps different than we were before.

In that spirit, a number of artists produced the works found in this book. Inspired by their own experiences with particular Psalms, these people of God give form to how the texts have spoken to them. As it should be, they vary considerably, multiple voices of faith collected under one roof.

I suspect that nothing in the Bible works as well as the Psalms with the practice of "bibliomancy," the practice of randomly opening it up to see what you may see. Often, I have found myself with a half an hour and no agenda, probably between things, so out has come the book, flipped open near the middle, and it has (sometimes) sung as it may. It is my hope that the pieces of art included herein will encourage and complement the same.

Many have noted over the centuries that Psalm 1 and Psalm 150 bookend the psalter, starting with a call to participation based on common sense (1:3 "They are like trees planted by streams of water") and concluding with sheer joy (150:6 "Let everything that breathes praise the Lord!"). We like it when life's wisdoms "work," but what we really want is to end in joy. Individually and collectively, the Psalms can address and transform our journeys. So be it.

Bill Maury-Holmes

Psalm 2 (NSRV)

1 Why do the nations conspire,
and the peoples plot in vain?
2 The kings of the earth set themselves,
and the rulers take counsel together,
against the LORD and his anointed, saying,
3 "Let us burst their bonds asunder,
and cast their cords from us."
4 He who sits in the heavens laughs,
the LORD has them in derision.
5 Then he will speak to them in his wrath,
and terrify them in his fury, saying,
6 "I have set my king on Zion, my holy hill."
7 I will tell of the decree of the LORD:
He said to me, "You are my son;
today I have begotten you.
8 Ask of me, and I will make the nations your heritage,
and the ends of the earth your possession.
9 You shall break them with a rod of iron,
and dash them in pieces like a potter's vessel."
10 Now therefore, O kings, be wise;
be warned, O rulers of the earth.
11 Serve the LORD with fear,
with trembling 12 kiss his feet,
or he will be angry, and you will perish in the way;
for his wrath is quickly kindled.
Happy are all who take refuge in him.

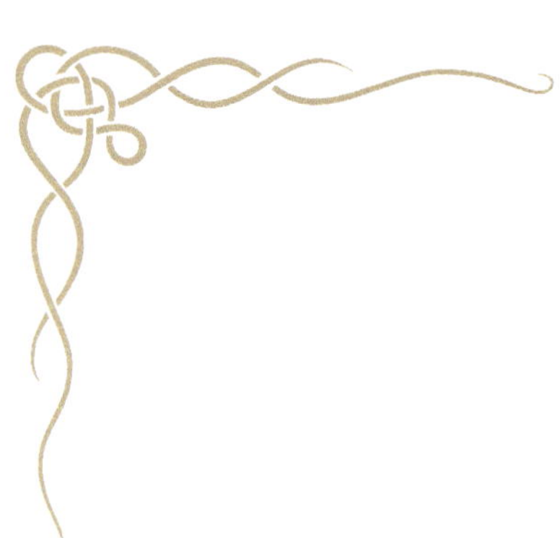

Photography tends to be a very literal art form. That is to say, while one could create abstract images, when illustrating something as beautiful and meaningful as the psalms, the simplest, most descriptive image is one which shows the lines as they are written. In this case, God's relationship with the psalmist is described as that of father and son. This photo aims to show the love and complexity of such a relationship: the son wanting to do right, and to be in his father's presence, and the father wanting to be the best guide and influence possible.

Larry Rose

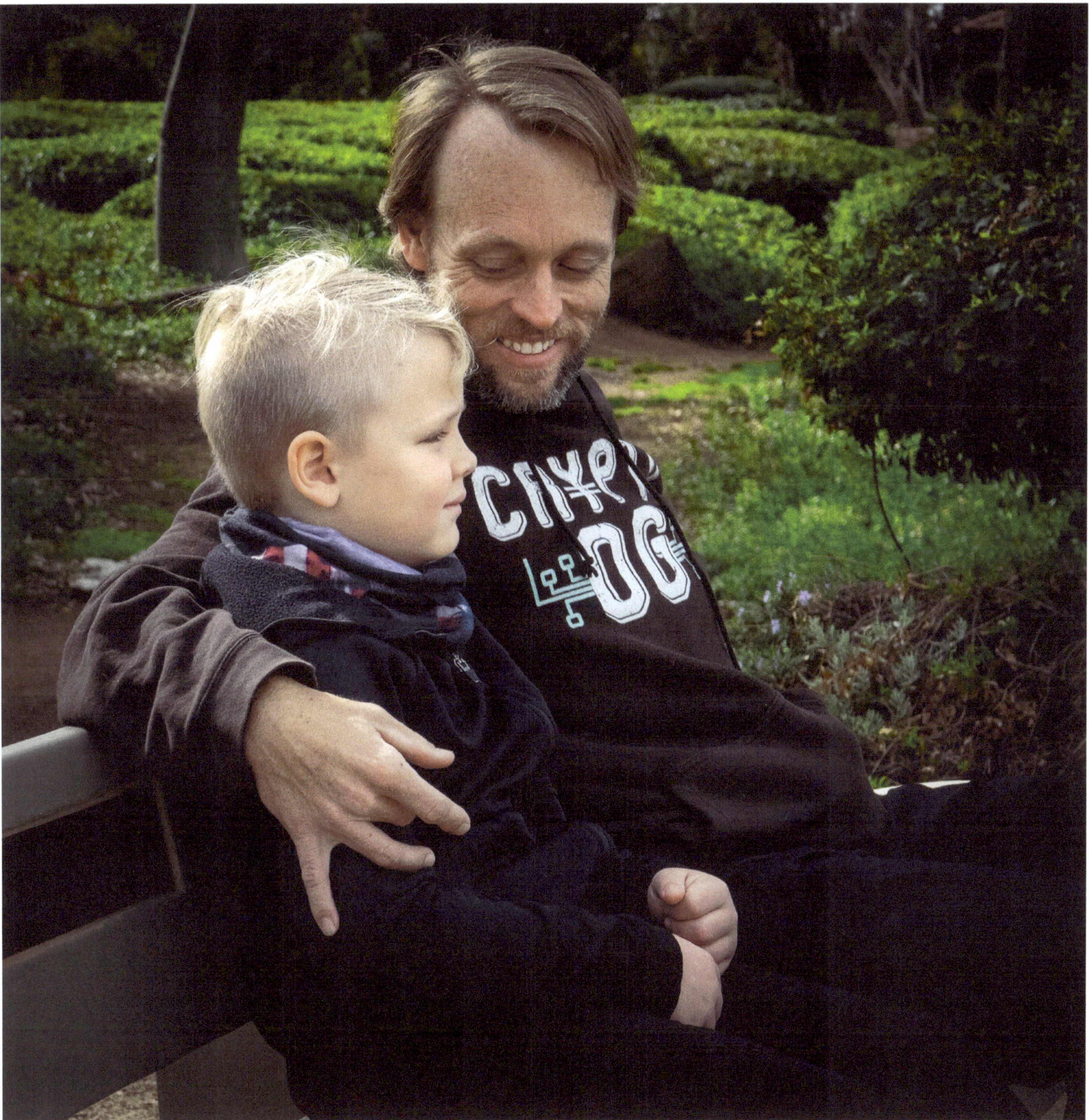

Psalm 8 (NSRV)

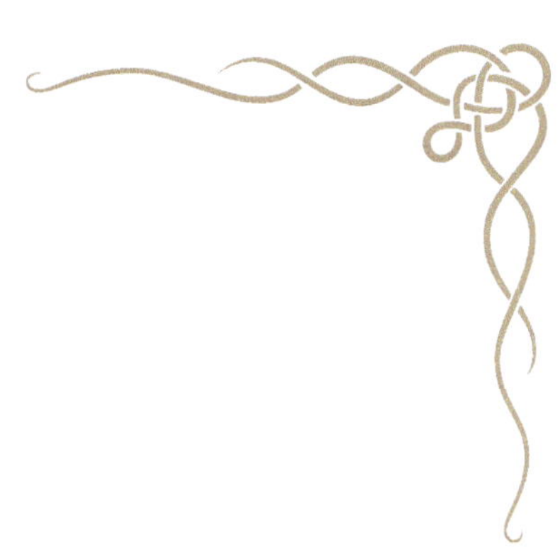

1 O Lord, our Sovereign,
how majestic is your name in all the earth!
You have set your glory above the heavens.
2 Out of the mouths of babes and infants
you have founded a bulwark because of your foes,
to silence the enemy and the avenger.
3 When I look at your heavens, the work of your fingers,
the moon and the stars that you have established;
4 what are human beings that you are mindful of them,
mortals that you care for them?
5 Yet you have made them a little lower than God,
and crowned them with glory and honor.
6 You have given them dominion over the works of your hands;
you have put all things under their feet,
7 all sheep and oxen,
and also the beasts of the field,
8 the birds of the air, and the fish of the sea,
whatever passes along the paths of the seas.
9 O Lord, our Sovereign,
how majestic is your name in all the earth!

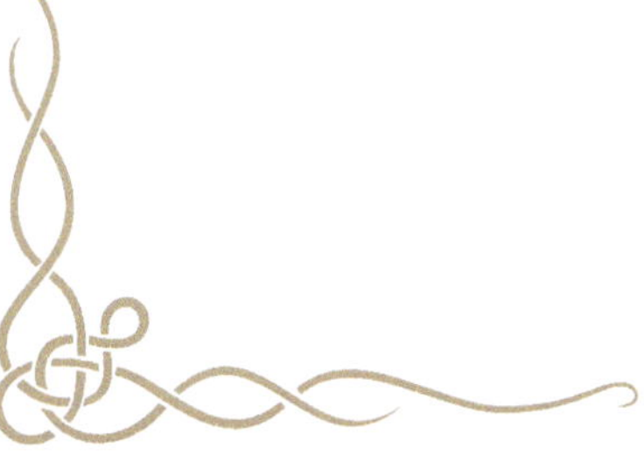

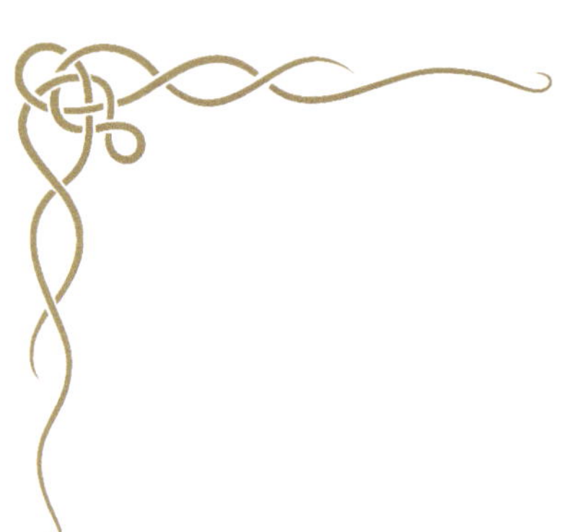

My mind went to the vastness of creation. That perspective is important when images go from mind to hand to heart. I was the little girl lying on her back looking at the stars, at the shore watching the ocean breathe, in the mountains standing among the giant trees. I chose to make the hands of God an unreal color so as not to be confused with human hands. I wanted the balance of the entire cycle of the moon and stars, of the light of day and the dark of night. My hope is that the viewer will feel both blessed and humble, while also experiencing gratitude at the wonder of creation.

Mary Melcher

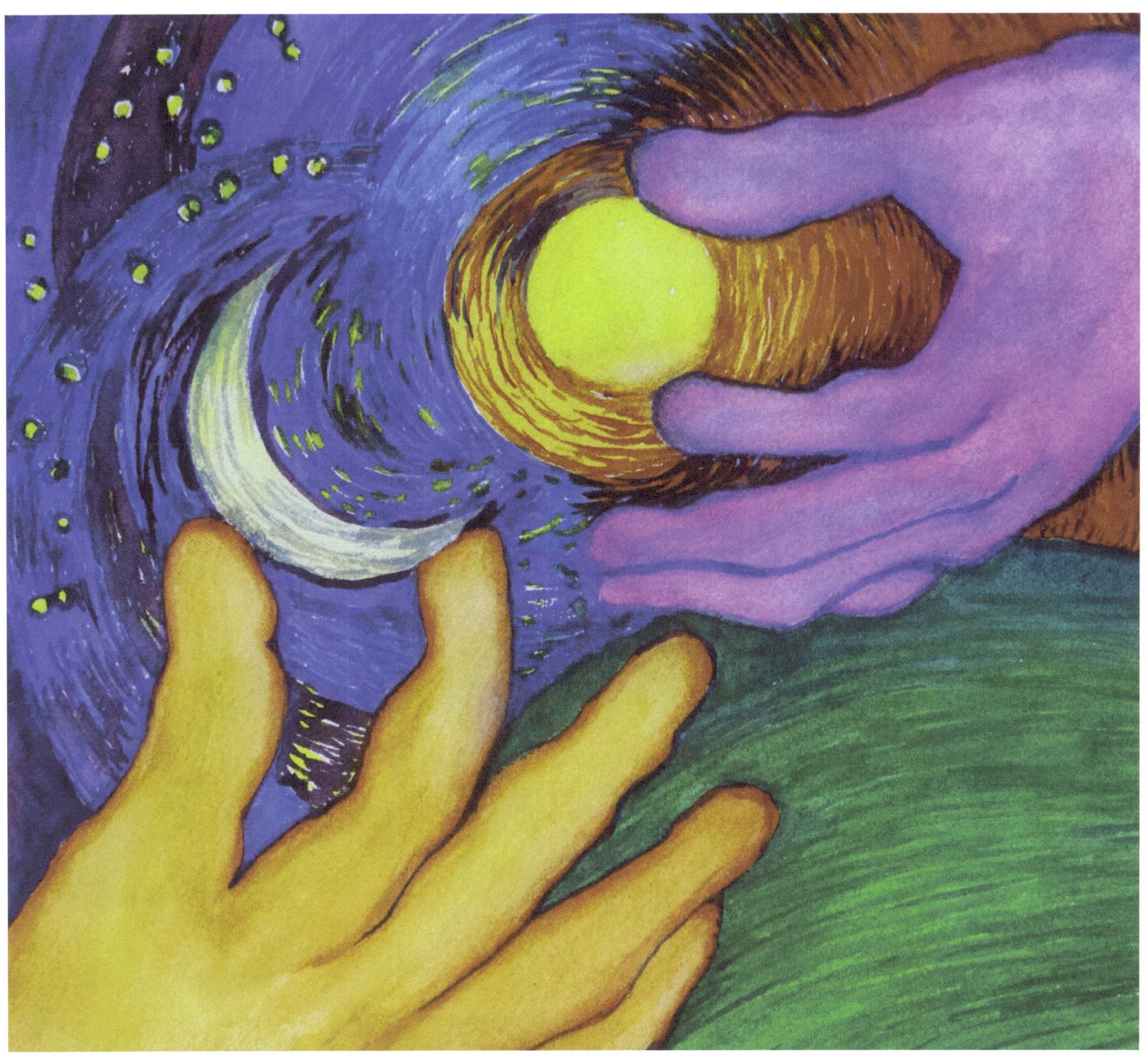

Psalm 8 echoes the thoughts and questions I think of when I gaze up at the massive, beautiful, starry night sky; all of the distant stars and galaxies dancing and shimmering in the heavens, like diamonds, sapphires, and rubies. Every time I look up at the magnificent night sky, I think to myself, Where do we fit into this puzzle called life? Can we be the only creatures in this immense universe? For what purpose were we created? How are there so many stars, planets, and galaxies out there, and who made them? Did someone just paint the night sky? Then, unexpectedly, a shooting star suddenly makes its mark across the jewel-filled sky, revealing to me that the night sky and the heavens are real and alive.

Drew Morgan

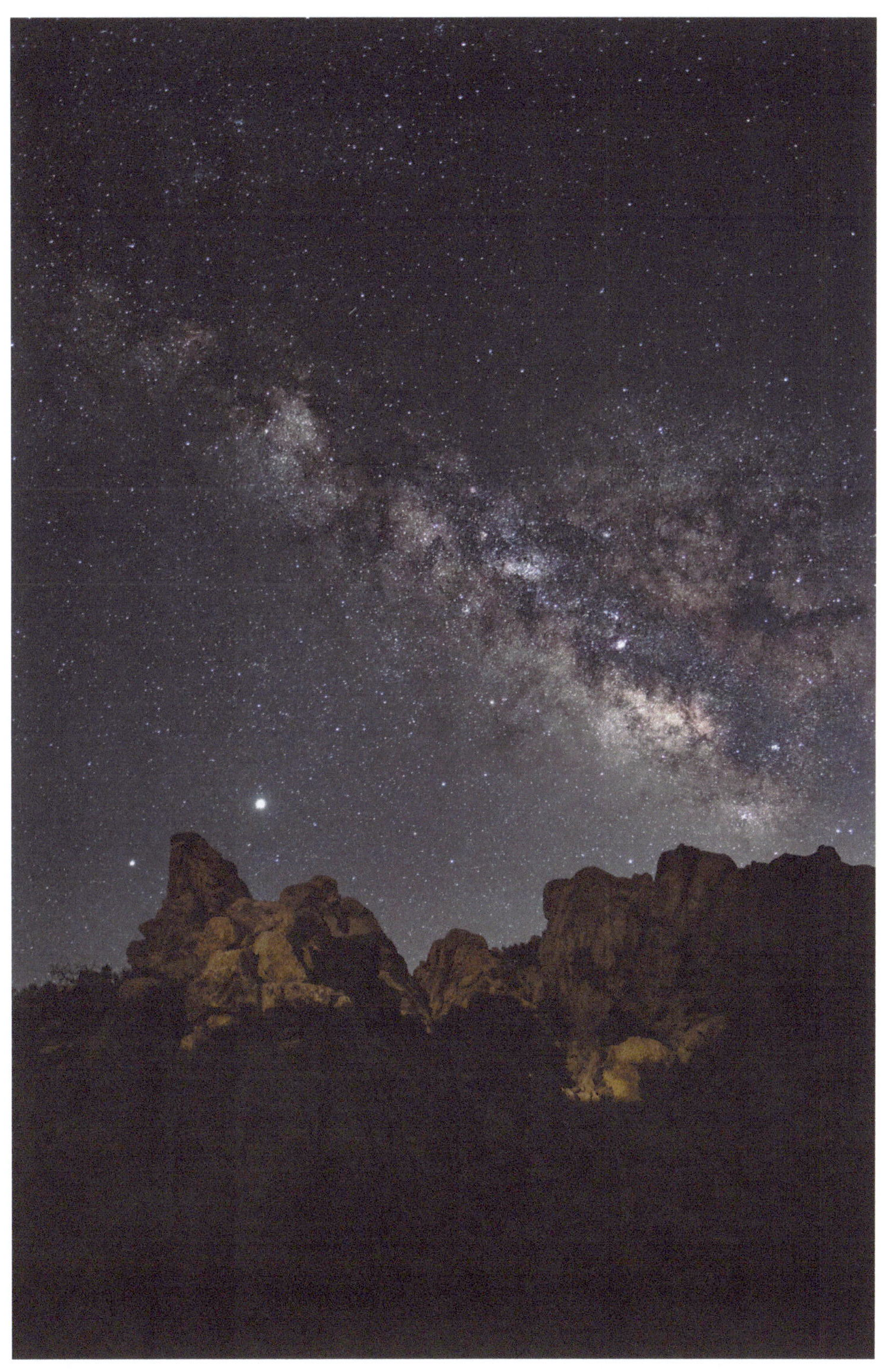

Psalm 19 (NSRV)

1 The heavens are telling the glory of God;
and the firmament proclaims his handiwork.
2 Day to day pours forth speech,
and night to night declares knowledge.
3 There is no speech, nor are there words;
their voice is not heard;
4 yet their voice goes out through all the earth,
and their words to the end of the world.
In the heavens he has set a tent for the sun,
5 which comes out like a bridegroom from his wedding canopy,
and like a strong man runs its course with joy.
6 Its rising is from the end of the heavens,
and its circuit to the end of them;
and nothing is hid from its heat.
7 The law of the LORD is perfect,
reviving the soul;
the decrees of the LORD are sure,
making wise the simple;
8 the precepts of the LORD are right,
rejoicing the heart;
the commandment of the LORD is clear,
enlightening the eyes;
9 the fear of the LORD is pure,
enduring forever;
the ordinances of the LORD are true
and righteous altogether.
10 More to be desired are they than gold,
even much fine gold;
sweeter also than honey,
and drippings of the honeycomb.

11 Moreover by them is your servant warned;
in keeping them there is great reward.
12 But who can detect their errors?
Clear me from hidden faults.
13 Keep back your servant also from the insolent;
do not let them have dominion over me.
Then I shall be blameless,
and innocent of great transgression.
14 Let the words of my mouth and the meditation of my heart be acceptable to you,
O LORD, my rock and my redeemer

It's the opening lines of the psalm which catch my attention and hold it in this instance. The idea of God's own handicraft being the very world we live in...well, it set the wheels of my imagination turning. Looking at the sky, the "heavens," has always made me feel closer to God. Sunset and sunrise are the times when I am perhaps most aware of the miracle of God's creation, with color upon color layered and patterned, never the same way twice. This is the "tent" that God has "pitched for the sun," the proclamation of the heavens.

Rev. Erin Beardemphl

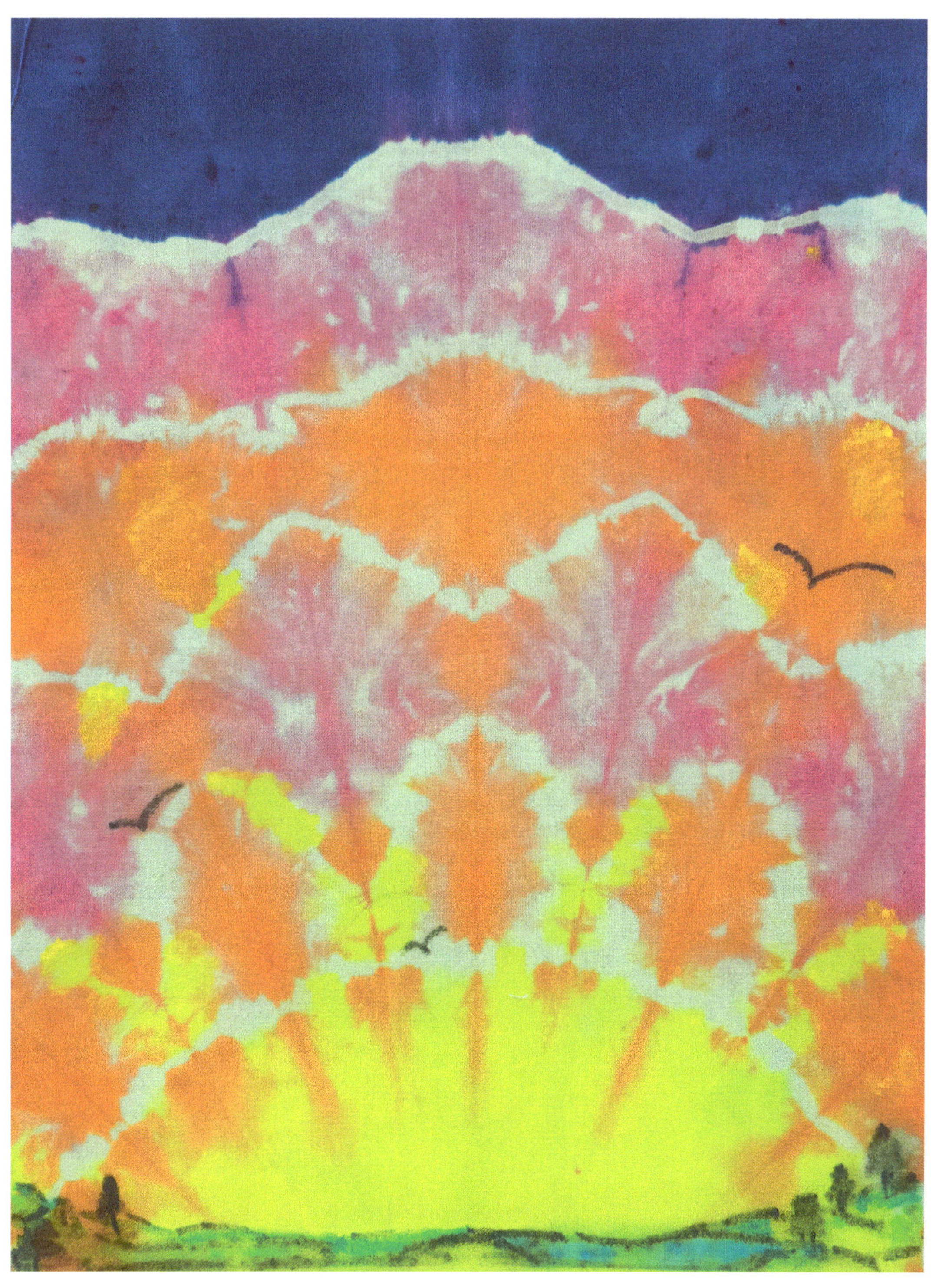

Psalm 23 (NSRV)

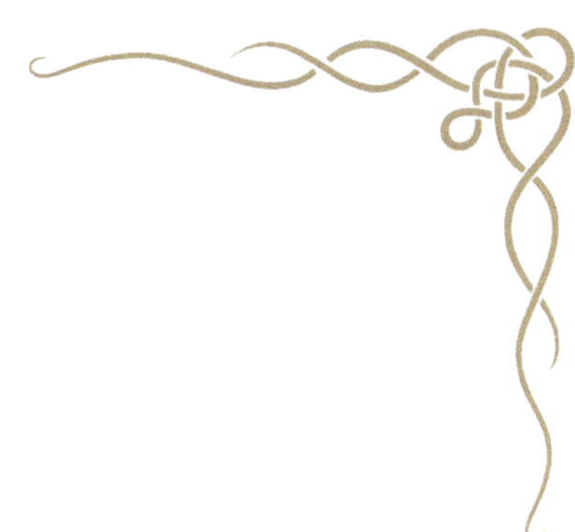

1 The LORD is my shepherd, I shall not want.
2   He makes me lie down in green pastures;
  he leads me beside still waters;
    3   he restores my soul.
  He leads me in right paths
    for his name's sake.
4 Even though I walk through the darkest valley,
  I fear no evil;
  for you are with me;
  your rod and your staff—
    they comfort me.
5 You prepare a table before me
  in the presence of my enemies;
  you anoint my head with oil;
    my cup overflows.
6 Surely goodness and mercy shall follow me
  all the days of my life,
and I shall dwell in the house of the LORD
    my whole life long.

This psalm has been illustrated again and again, gracing the halls of churches and synagogues, funeral homes, and even the walls of children's nurseries. These images frequently involve a shepherd (in Christian circles, it is often a European looking Jesus shepherd), sheep, a green field with water running... And many of us have seen these so often that they are the first pictures that come to mind when we ponder the familiar lines. However, as I studied this psalm afresh with my church community in the midst of 2020 chaos, the familiar images no longer served their purpose. As a viral pandemic swirled around us and blatant racism cracked our sense of safety and justice, hope showed me a light at the end of the tunnel, but I found myself identifying most with the "shadow of the valley of death" rather than the green pastures or the cool waters. And so I began to lay my piece, first dyes, then paints; a brightly colored square of fabric, quickly covered in the dark walls of our narrow valley, with that light at the end of the tunnel poking through. Perhaps, on the other side of this experience, I will look toward the pastoral landscapes again. For now, I stand in the crevice, looking toward the light of hope.

Rev. Erin Beardemphl

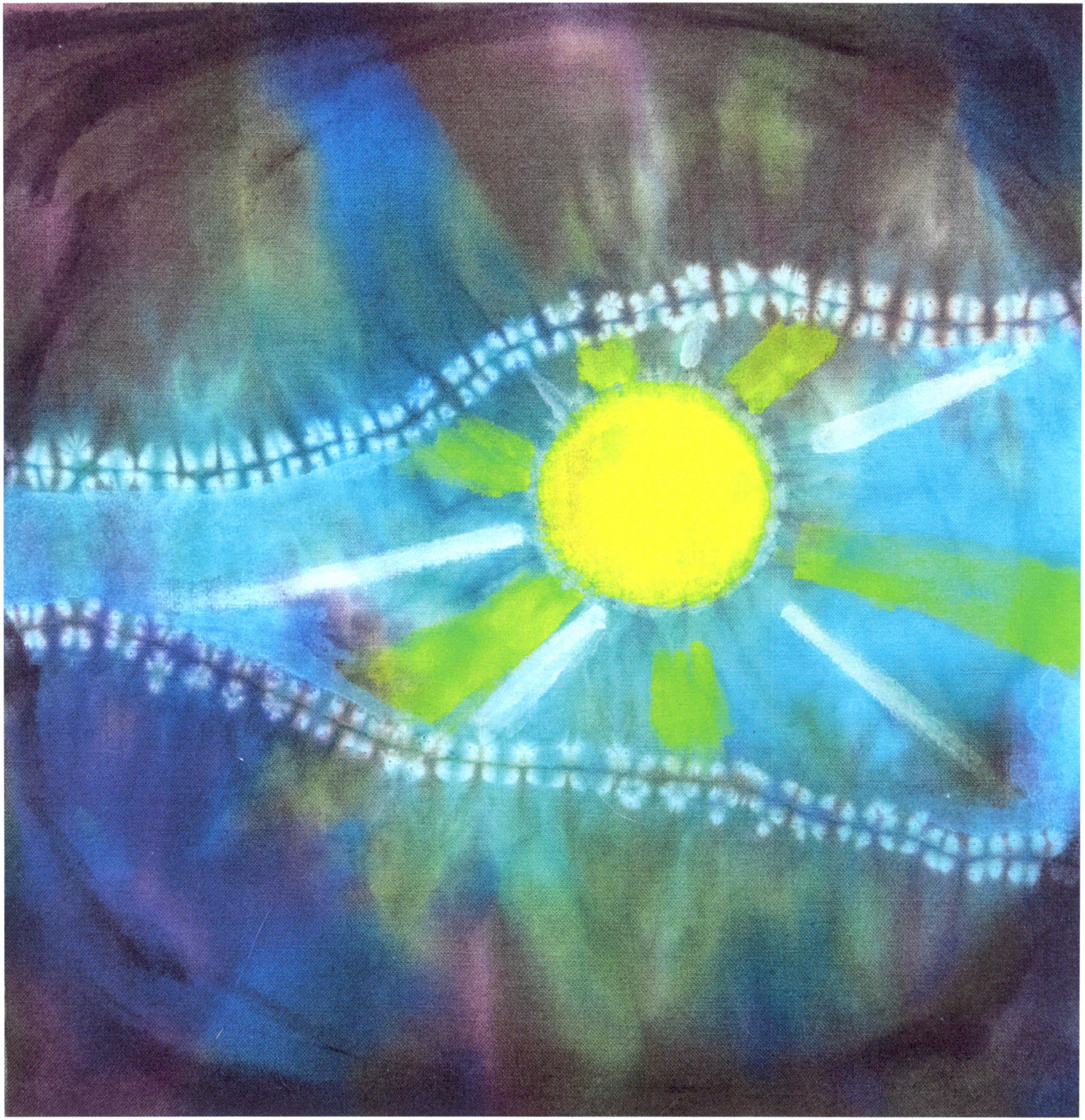

Psalm 24 (NSRV)

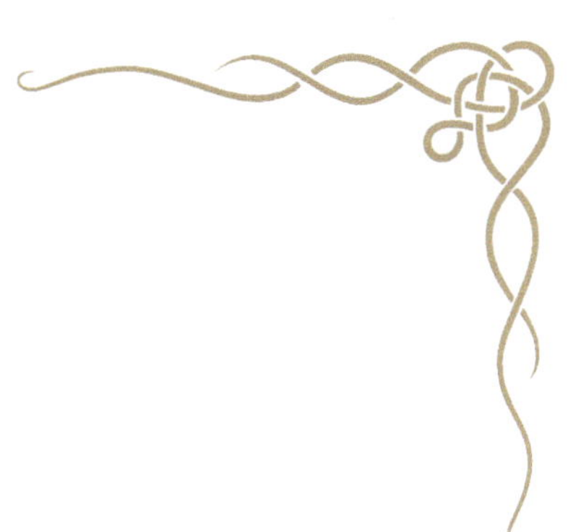

1 The earth is the LORD's and all that is in it,
    the world, and those who live in it;
2 for he has founded it on the seas,
    and established it on the rivers.
3 Who shall ascend the hill of the LORD?
    And who shall stand in his holy place?
4 Those who have clean hands and pure hearts,
    who do not lift up their souls to what is false,
        and do not swear deceitfully.
5 They will receive blessing from the LORD,
    and vindication from the God of their salvation.
6 Such is the company of those who seek him,
    who seek the face of the God of Jacob.[a]Selah

    7 Lift up your heads, O gates!
    and be lifted up, O ancient doors!
    that the King of glory may come in.
    8 Who is the King of glory?
    The LORD, strong and mighty,
        the LORD, mighty in battle.
9 Lift up your heads, O gates!
    and be lifted up, O ancient doors!
    that the King of glory may come in.
10 Who is this King of glory?
    The LORD of hosts,
        he is the King of glory. Selah

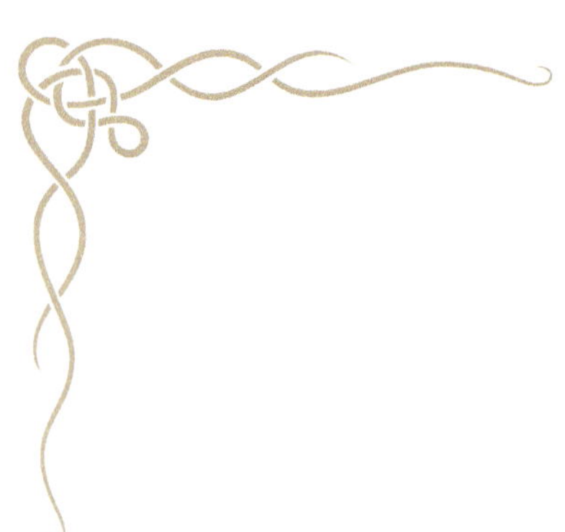

So wake up, you living gateways!
Lift up your heads, you ageless
 doors of destiny!
Welcome the King of Glory,
for he is about to come through you.
You ask, "Who is this Glory-King?"
 The Lord, armed and ready for battle,
the Mighty One, invincible in every way!
So wake up, you living gateways, and rejoice!
Fling wide, you ageless doors of destiny!
Here he comes; the King of Glory is
 ready to come in.
You ask, "Who is this King of Glory?"
He is the Lord of Victory, armed and
 ready for battle,
the Mighty One, the invincible commander
 of heaven's hosts!
Yes, he is the King of Glory!
Pause in his presence

Cindy R.

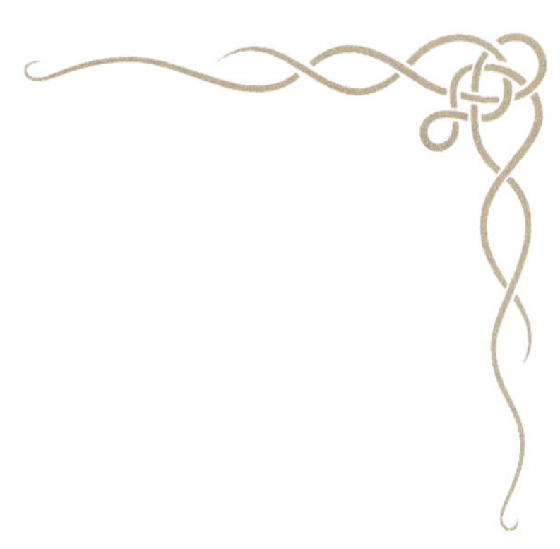

Living gateways. So many doors.
Which do you choose? When?
Active. Pulsing. Pause in the presence.

Whale welcomes the journey. Wolf sings
of dreams woven and birthed. Mother
Mary cradles the balance between plants,
animals, humans in Earth and Sky.

Stars, sun, and moon shine on all of us.
Deer holds love in his antlers. You meditate
on stardust with butterfly and moth. Drink
herbs to heal and wait until doors fling wide.

Rejoice, heavenly hosts.
The presence. The Glory!

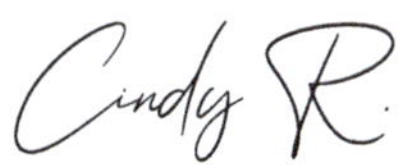

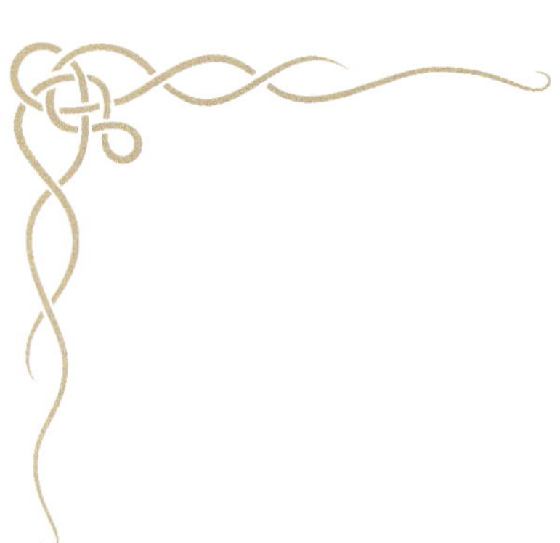

Living gateways and doors of destiny excite me. There are times when I need the Divine to stand as protector. But my vision of a King of Glory has expanded to include many faith traditions – goddesses, shamans, mystics, nature, stillness, mindfulness, movement, breath, and more. These are what sustain and encourage me on the journey.

Cindy Rinne

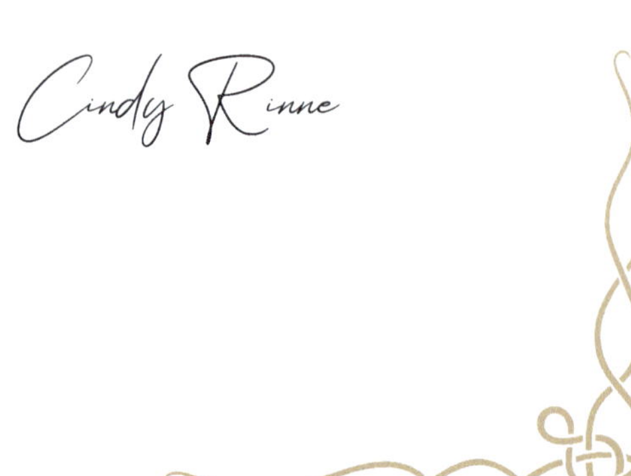

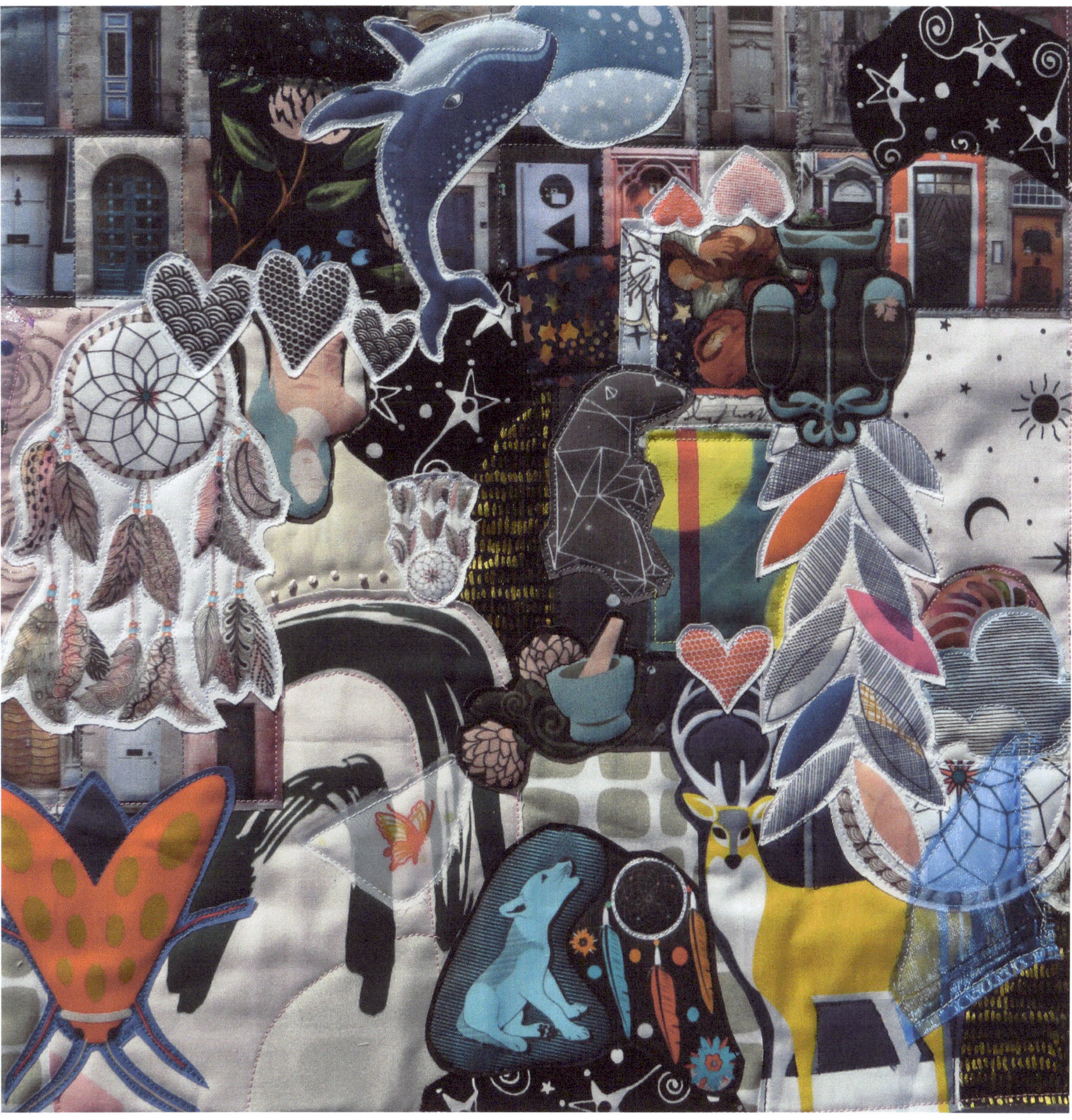

Psalm 30 _(NSRV)

1 I will extol you, O LORD, for you have drawn me up,
and did not let my foes rejoice over me.
2 O LORD my God, I cried to you for help,
and you have healed me.
3 O LORD, you brought up my soul from Sheol,
restored me to life from among those gone down to the Pit.
4 Sing praises to the LORD, O you his faithful ones,
and give thanks to his holy name.
5 For his anger is but for a moment;
his favor is for a lifetime.
Weeping may linger for the night,
but joy comes with the morning.
6 As for me, I said in my prosperity,
"I shall never be moved."
7 By your favor, O LORD,
you had established me as a strong mountain;
you hid your face;
I was dismayed.
8 To you, O LORD, I cried,
and to the LORD I made supplication:
9 "What profit is there in my death,
if I go down to the Pit?
Will the dust praise you?
Will it tell of your faithfulness?
10 Hear, O LORD, and be gracious to me!
O LORD, be my helper!"
11 You have turned my mourning into dancing;
you have taken off my sackcloth
and clothed me with joy,
12 so that my soul may praise you and not be silent.
O LORD my God, I will give thanks to you forever.

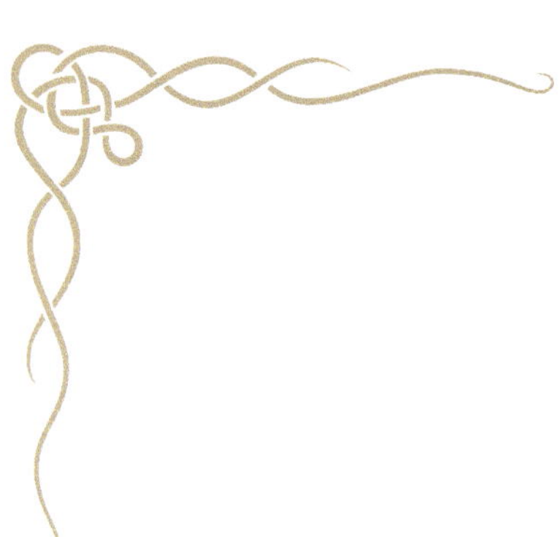

Showing the changing of emotion from tears and grief to joy and celebration in a single image is the challenge here. Although the transition from the evening's sadness to the morning's life-giving delight leaves a memory of sorrow, it also lifts up life and all its possibilities. This image aims to show the presence of both, though God's joy is the stronger of the two.

Larry Rose

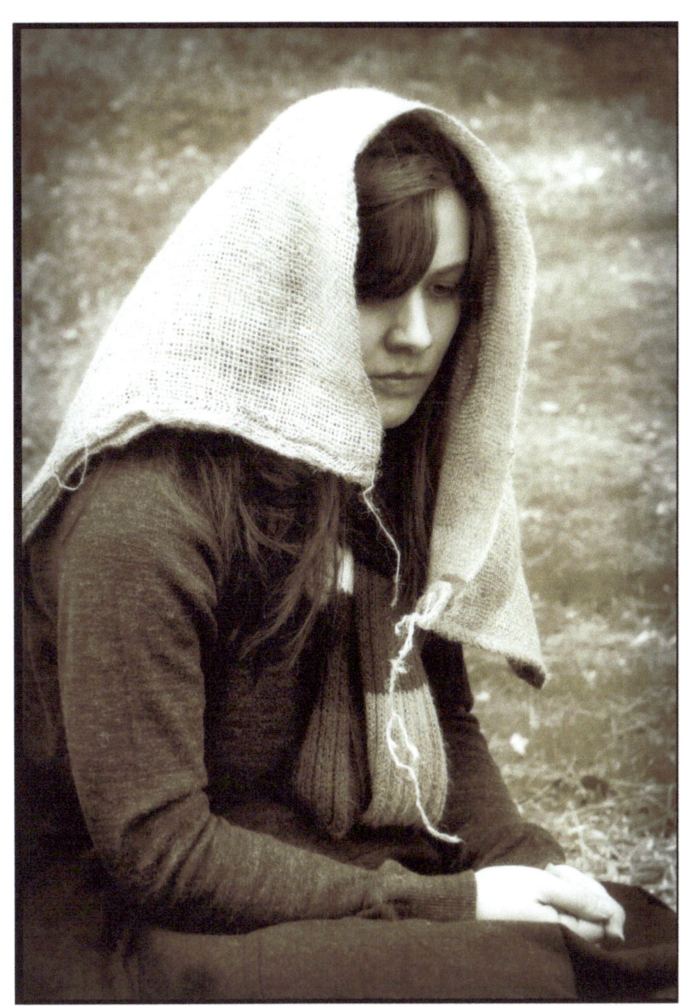
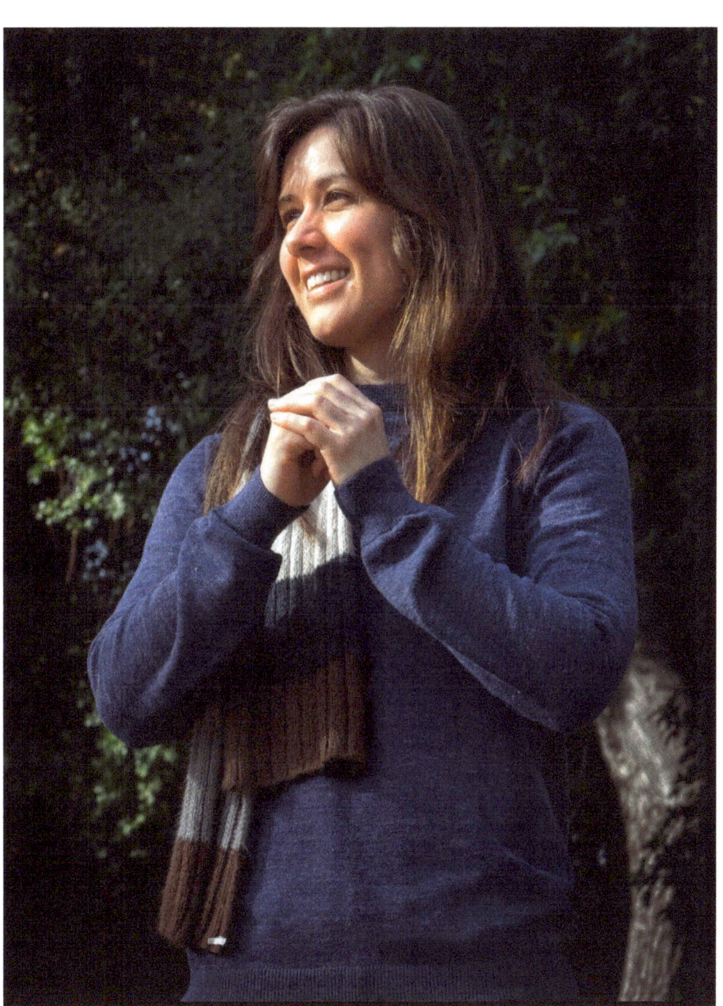

Psalm 32 (MSG)

1 Count yourself lucky, how happy you must be—
you get a fresh start,
your slate's wiped clean.
2 Count yourself lucky—
GOD holds nothing against you
and you're holding nothing back from him.
3 When I kept it all inside,
my bones turned to powder,
my words became daylong groans.
4 The pressure never let up;
all the juices of my life dried up.
5 Then I let it all out;
I said, "I'll come clean about my failures to GOD."
Suddenly the pressure was gone—
my guilt dissolved,
my sin disappeared.
6 These things add up. Every one of us needs to pray;
when all hell breaks loose and the dam bursts
we'll be on high ground, untouched.
7 GOD's my island hideaway,
keeps danger far from the shore,
throws garlands of hosannas around my neck.
8 Let me give you some good advice;
I'm looking you in the eye
and giving it to you straight:
9 "Don't be ornery like a horse or mule
that needs bit and bridle
to stay on track."

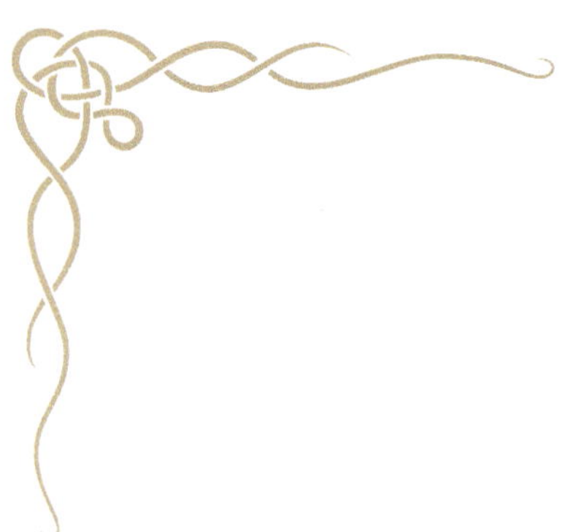

Psalm 32 speaks of resentments, reflection, and
release through confession.

"God holds nothing against you and you're
holding nothing back from God." I was moved
by the reflection of trees and sky in the water,
how they were both extensions of each other.
The branches—the roots—the sky—the water.
The divine is both inside and outside oneself.
To deny this truth and hold everything in is to
thirst. Water and trees are universal symbols of
life, growth, and renewal.

Jessica Lea

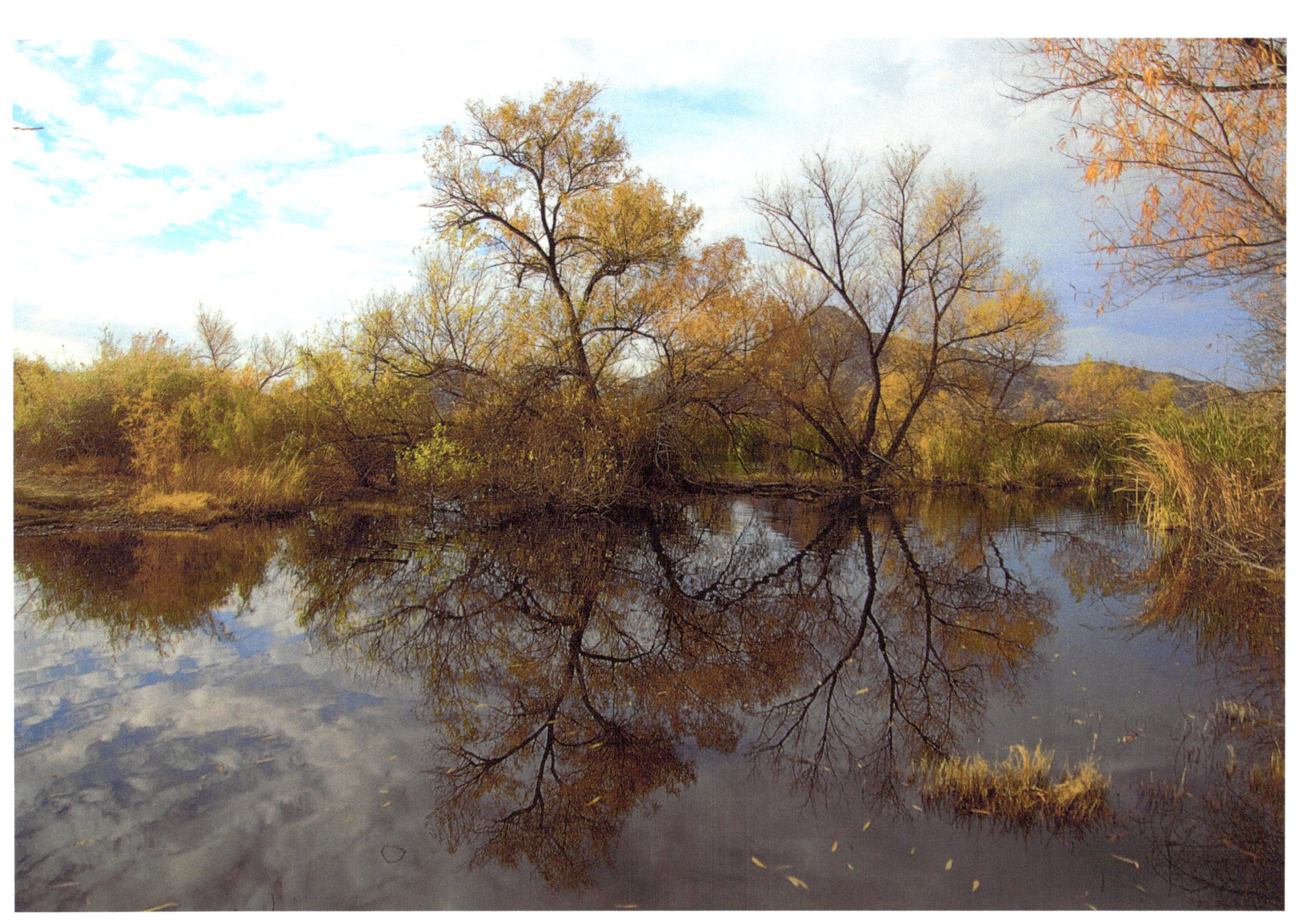

Psalm 33 (NSRV)

1 Rejoice in the LORD, O you righteous.
Praise befits the upright.
2 Praise the LORD with the lyre;
make melody to him with the harp of ten strings.
3 Sing to him a new song;
play skillfully on the strings, with loud shouts.
4 For the word of the LORD is upright,
and all his work is done in faithfulness.
5 He loves righteousness and justice;
the earth is full of the steadfast love of the LORD.
6 By the word of the LORD the heavens were made,
and all their host by the breath of his mouth.
7 He gathered the waters of the sea as in a bottle;
he put the deeps in storehouses.
8 Let all the earth fear the LORD;
let all the inhabitants of the world stand in awe of him.
9 For he spoke, and it came to be;
he commanded, and it stood firm.
10 The LORD brings the counsel of the nations to nothing;
he frustrates the plans of the peoples.
11 The counsel of the LORD stands forever,
the thoughts of his heart to all generations.
12 Happy is the nation whose God is the LORD,
the people whom he has chosen as his heritage.
13 The LORD looks down from heaven;
he sees all humankind.
14 From where he sits enthroned he watches
all the inhabitants of the earth—
15 he who fashions the hearts of them all,
and observes all their deeds.
16 A king is not saved by his great army;
a warrior is not delivered by his great strength.

17 The war horse is a vain hope for victory,
and by its great might it cannot save.
18 Truly the eye of the LORD is on those who fear him,
on those who hope in his steadfast love,
19 to deliver their soul from death,
and to keep them alive in famine.
20 Our soul waits for the LORD;
he is our help and shield.
21 Our heart is glad in him,
because we trust in his holy name.
22 Let your steadfast love, O LORD, be upon us,
even as we hope in you.

The psalmist pleads with God to keep the people alive in a famine - not to be well fed, or to be saved ahead of their enemies, but to simply live through it until their fortune is improved. This humble plea does not ask for grand or dramatic miracles, but for just enough to get by. "Truly the eye of the Lord is on... those who hope in his steadfast love." These are the words of a people reaching out to God, not to show how faithful they are, or to gain status within their community, but to keep their part of a covenant where God promises to be the people's own, and the people promise to be God's own. From this mutual love, surviving becomes thriving, and God and the people endure together.

Rev. Erin Beardemphl

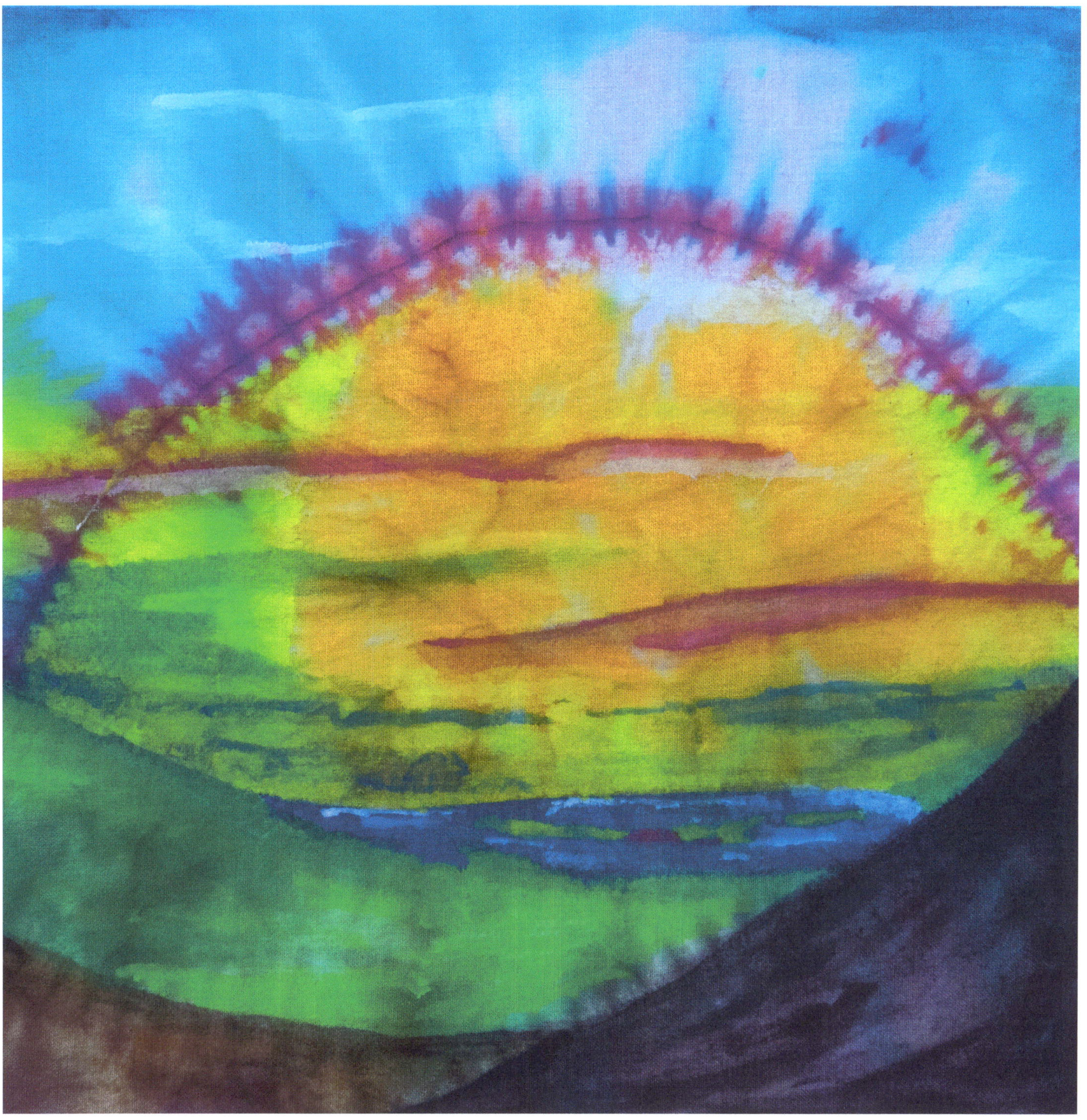

Psalm 43 (NSRV)

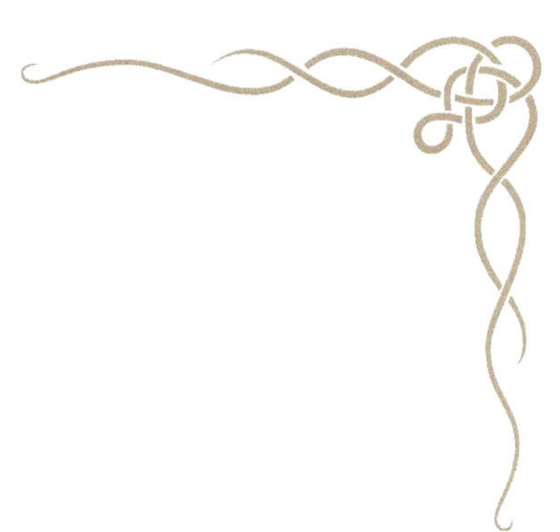

1 Vindicate me, O God, and defend my cause
against an ungodly people;
from those who are deceitful and unjust
deliver me!
2 For you are the God in whom I take refuge;
why have you cast me off?
Why must I walk about mournfully
because of the oppression of the enemy?
3 O send out your light and your truth;
let them lead me;
let them bring me to your holy hill
and to your dwelling.
4 Then I will go to the altar of God,
to God my exceeding joy;
and I will praise you with the harp,
O God, my God.
5 Why are you cast down, O my soul,
and why are you disquieted within me?
Hope in God; for I shall again praise him,
my help and my God.

This piece is one of two that was inspired during a retreat and respite at a hermitage in Big Sur. It is meant to show the wonder of slipping from Chronos time into Kairos time; it is a moment of grace where I feel God is close. I mostly loved the unworldly light that I experienced in that space.

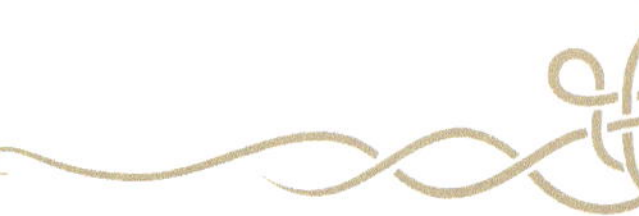

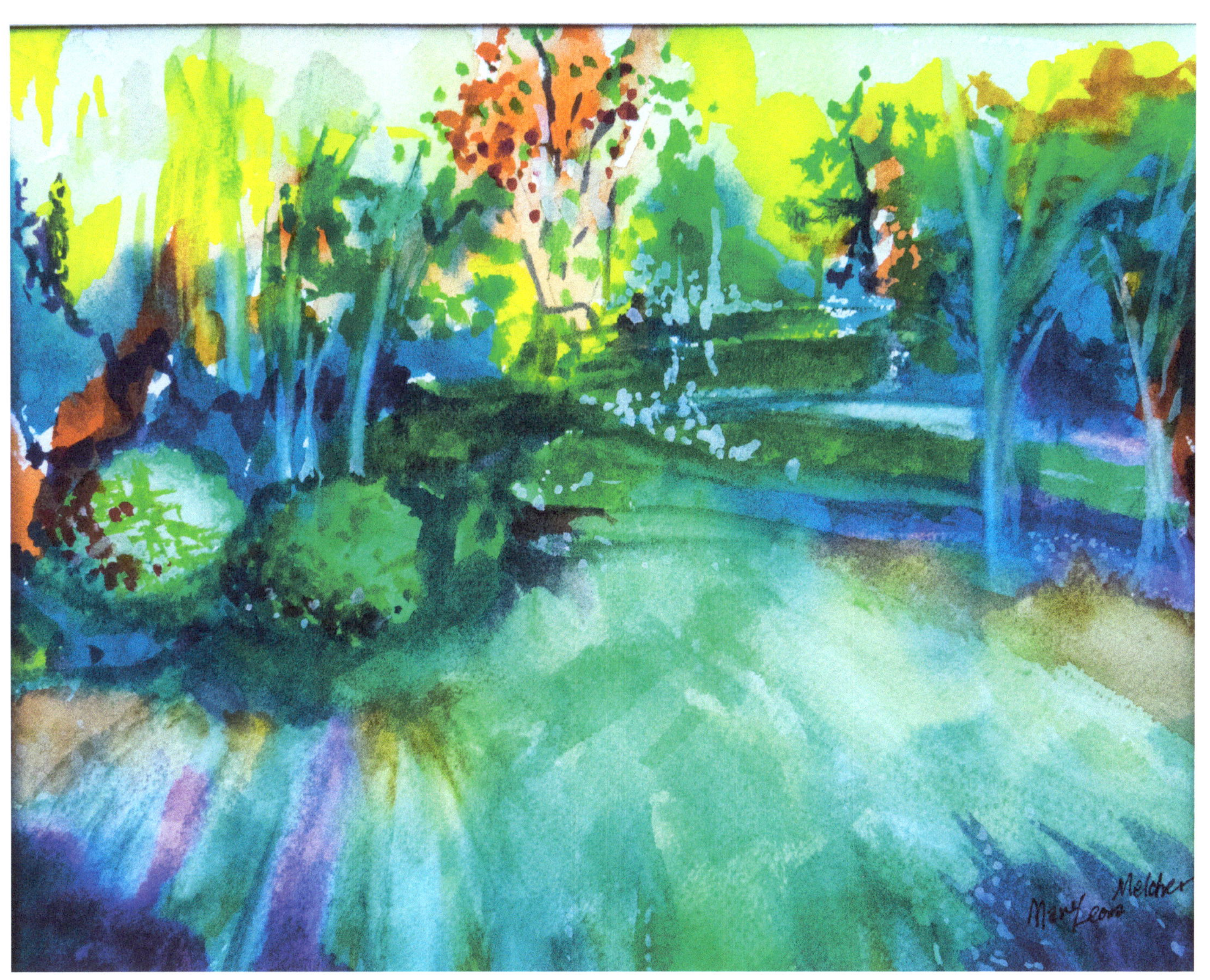
Mary Leona Melcher

Psalm 46 (NSRV)

1 God is our refuge and strength,
a very present help in trouble.
2 Therefore we will not fear, though the earth should change,
though the mountains shake in the heart of the sea;
3 though its waters roar and foam,
though the mountains tremble with its tumult.Selah
4 There is a river whose streams make glad the city of God,
the holy habitation of the Most High.
5 God is in the midst of the city; it shall not be moved;
God will help it when the morning dawns.
6 The nations are in an uproar, the kingdoms totter;
he utters his voice, the earth melts.
7 The Lord of hosts is with us;
the God of Jacob is our refuge.Selah
8 Come, behold the works of the Lord;
see what desolations he has brought on the earth.
9 He makes wars cease to the end of the earth;
he breaks the bow, and shatters the spear;
he burns the shields with fire.
10 "Be still, and know that I am God!
I am exalted among the nations,
I am exalted in the earth."
11 The Lord of hosts is with us;
the God of Jacob is our refuge.Selah

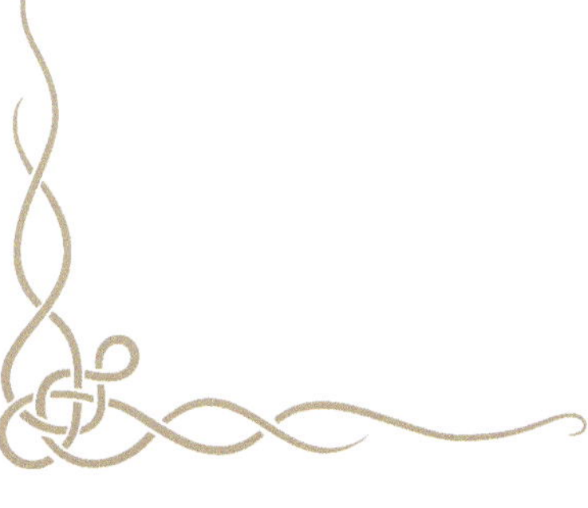

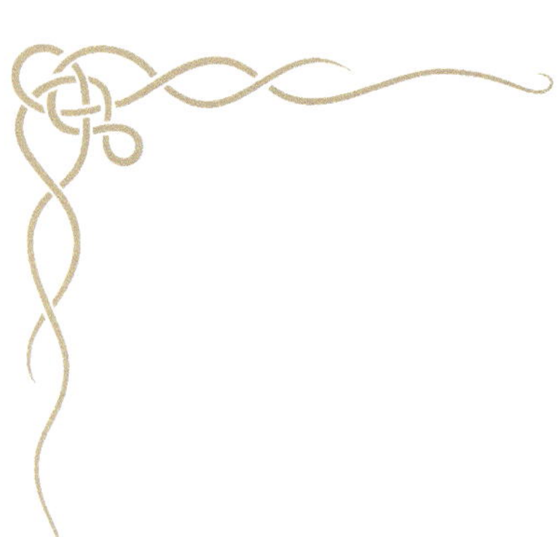

Rivers are important teachers of this life on earth. They nurture the land and it's plants and animals. They serve as a meeting place for people, teaching them to go with the flow. Water can be both powerful and dangerous and is ever changing even as it transforms life.

Mary Melcher

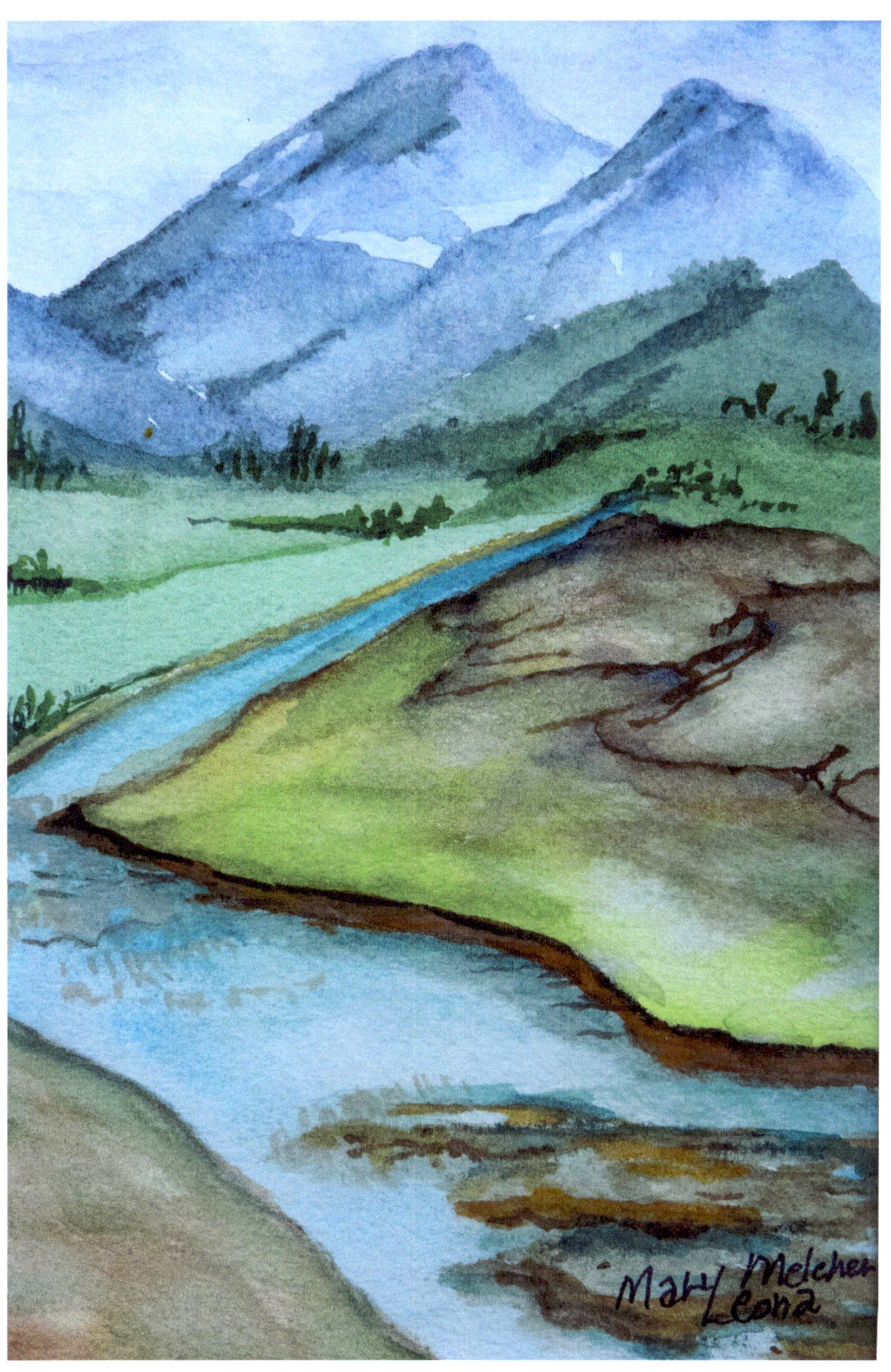

Mary Melchen
Leona

Psalm 80 (NSRV)

1 Give ear, O Shepherd of Israel,
    you who lead Joseph like a flock!
You who are enthroned upon the cherubim, shine forth
2   before Ephraim and Benjamin and Manasseh.
        Stir up your might,
          and come to save us!
        3 Restore us, O God;
    let your face shine, that we may be saved.
        4 O LORD God of hosts,
how long will you be angry with your people's prayers?
    5 You have fed them with the bread of tears,
      and given them tears to drink in full measure.
      6 You make us the scorn of our neighbors;
          our enemies laugh among themselves.
        7 Restore us, O God of hosts;
    let your face shine, that we may be saved.
      8 You brought a vine out of Egypt;
      you drove out the nations and planted it.
        9 You cleared the ground for it;
        it took deep root and filled the land.
  10 The mountains were covered with its shade,
          the mighty cedars with its branches;
      11 it sent out its branches to the sea,
            and its shoots to the River.
  12 Why then have you broken down its walls,
  so that all who pass along the way pluck its fruit?
        13 The boar from the forest ravages it,
        and all that move in the field feed on it.

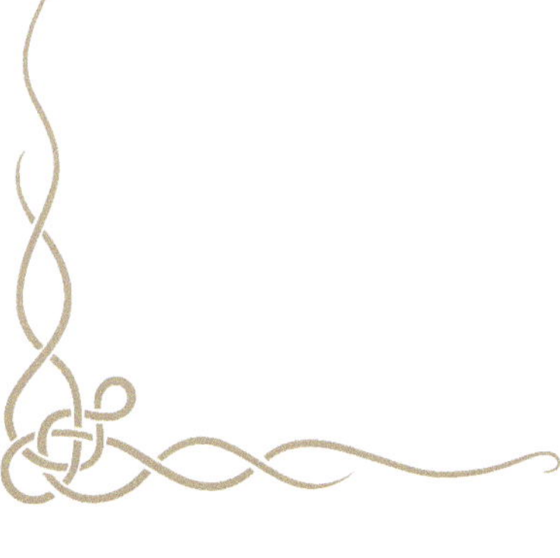

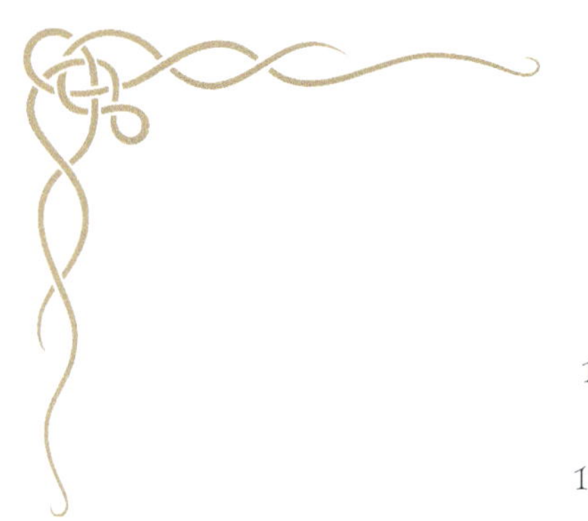

14 Turn again, O God of hosts;
look down from heaven, and see;
have regard for this vine,
15   the stock that your right hand planted.
16 They have burned it with fire, they have cut it down;
may they perish at the rebuke of your countenance.
17 But let your hand be upon the one at your right hand,
the one whom you made strong for yourself.
18 Then we will never turn back from you;
give us life, and we will call on your name.
19 Restore us, O LORD God of hosts;
let your face shine, that we may be saved.

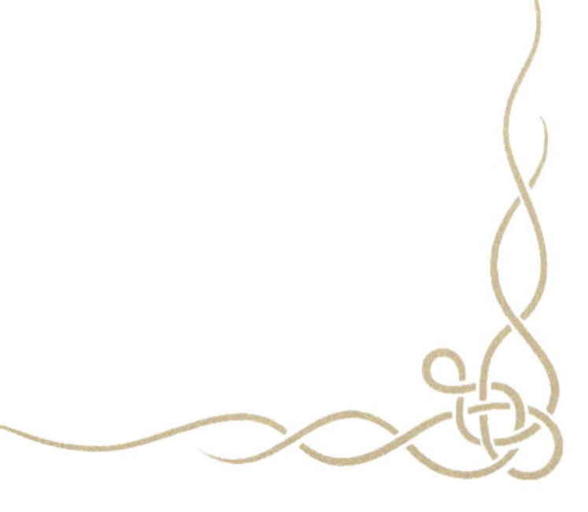

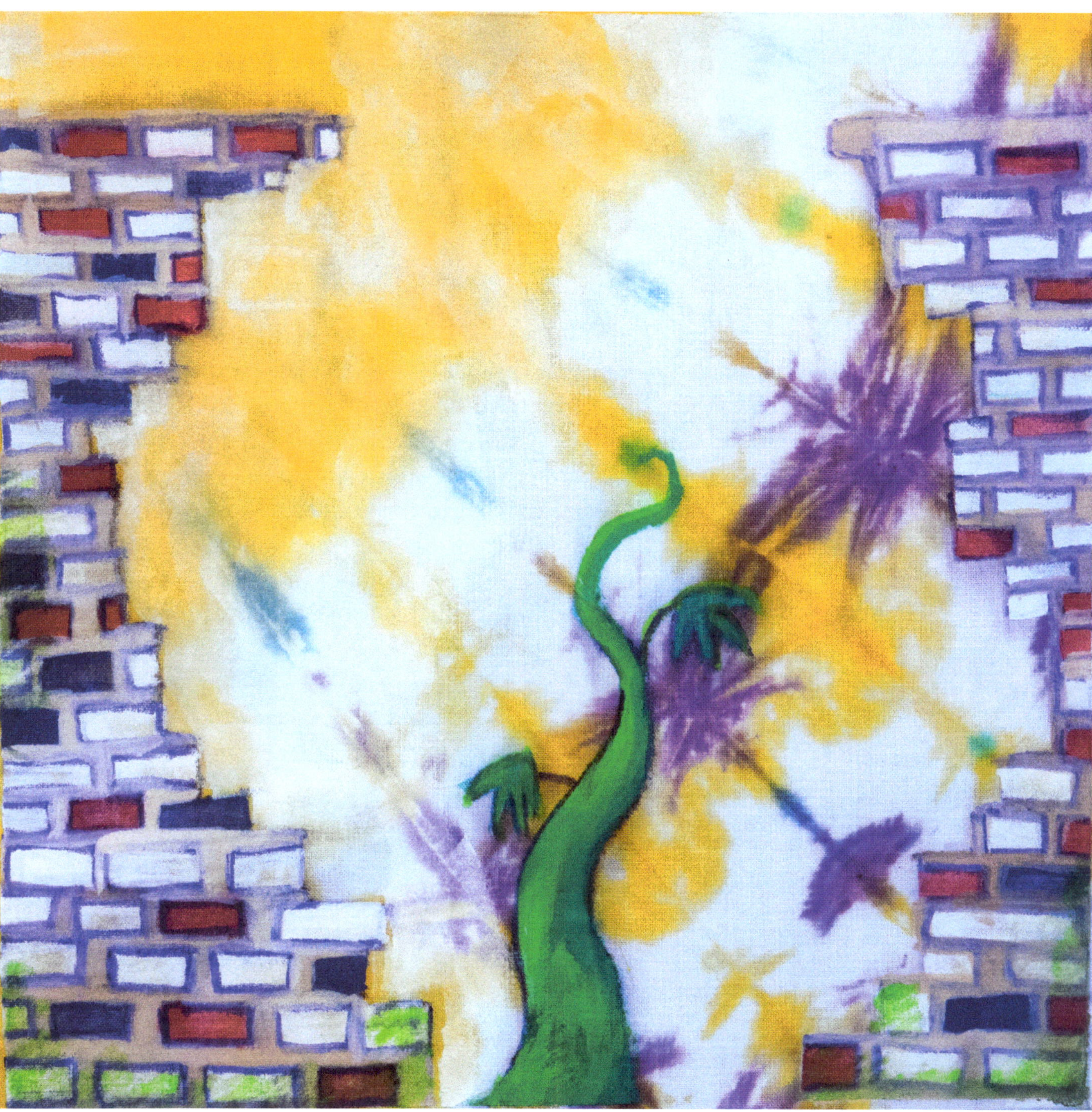

During a particularly bad heat wave last summer, I watched in frustration as the vines I had planted earlier that spring began to wilt and wither right before my eyes. I had taken great pains to keep hungry insects away, and had a routine of watering their bases every morning, but as the temperature continued to rise, the leaves began to crisp, the stems started to bend over, and the insects I had so far kept at bay began to invade despite my best efforts. I thought of this as I prepared for this psalm. It presents images of a grape vine no longer protected, suffering as predators cause damage and drying to a crisp in weather no longer suitable for its livelihood.

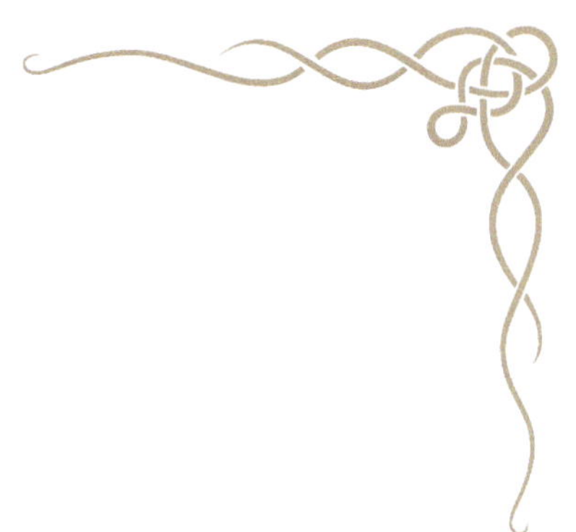

What must it feel like to be abandoned? The chorus of "Restore us, O God; let your faith shine, that we might be saved," became the focus for me as I thought about the shade I set over my suffering garden, the additional water I added to the soil, and the small dishes of water I left around to tempt the insects away from the plants. The burnt leaves would never recover, but new leaves budded and grew. Eventually, flowers joined the leaves and the bees and butterflies came. I thought, "Perhaps this is what restoration looks like!"- the new growth, the hope of flowers, the strength of what survived before. This new life starts out so slowly, and without patience, you may never be able to appreciate what is happening, but with the faith of what came before, it turns out that much is possible.

Rev. Erin Beardemphl

Psalm 82 (MSG)

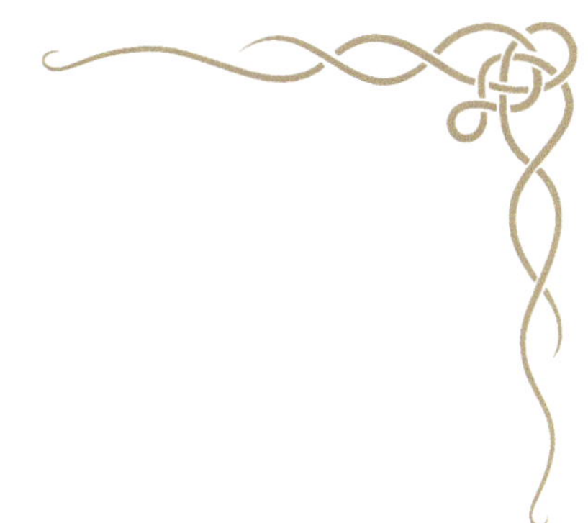

God calls the judges into his courtroom,
    he puts all the judges in the dock.
2-4 "Enough! You've corrupted justice long enough,
    you've let the wicked get away with murder.
You're here to defend the defenseless,
    to make sure that underdogs get a fair break;
Your job is to stand up for the powerless,
    and prosecute all those who exploit them."
5 Ignorant judges! Head-in-the-sand judges!
    They haven't a clue to what's going on.
And now everything's falling apart,
    the world's coming unglued.
6-7 "I appointed you judges, each one of you,
    deputies of the High God,
But you've betrayed your commission
    and now you're stripped of your rank, busted."
8 O God, give them what they've got coming!
    You've got the whole world in your hands!

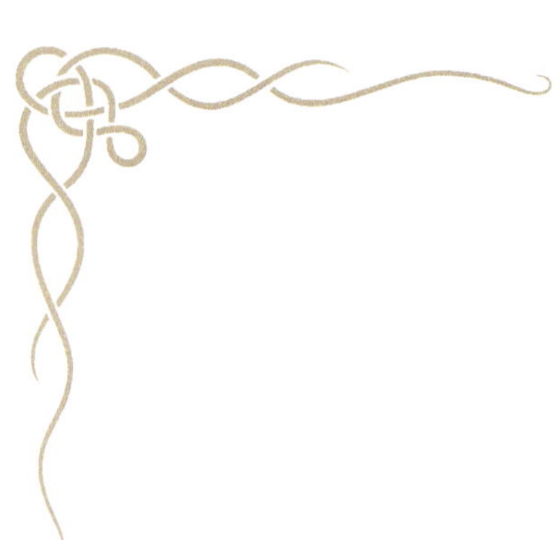

Psalm 82 is about using power to help others. "You're here to defend the defenseless...And now everything's coming apart. The world's coming unglued." The inverted scales of justice hold the world as it strains under pressures caused by injustices and strident disagreements. The pattern around the circle is part of Justice Ruth Bader Ginsberg's dissent collar. She is a personal role model and her absence is keenly felt as my country tries to regain its balance. The butterfly brings hope.

Jessica Lea

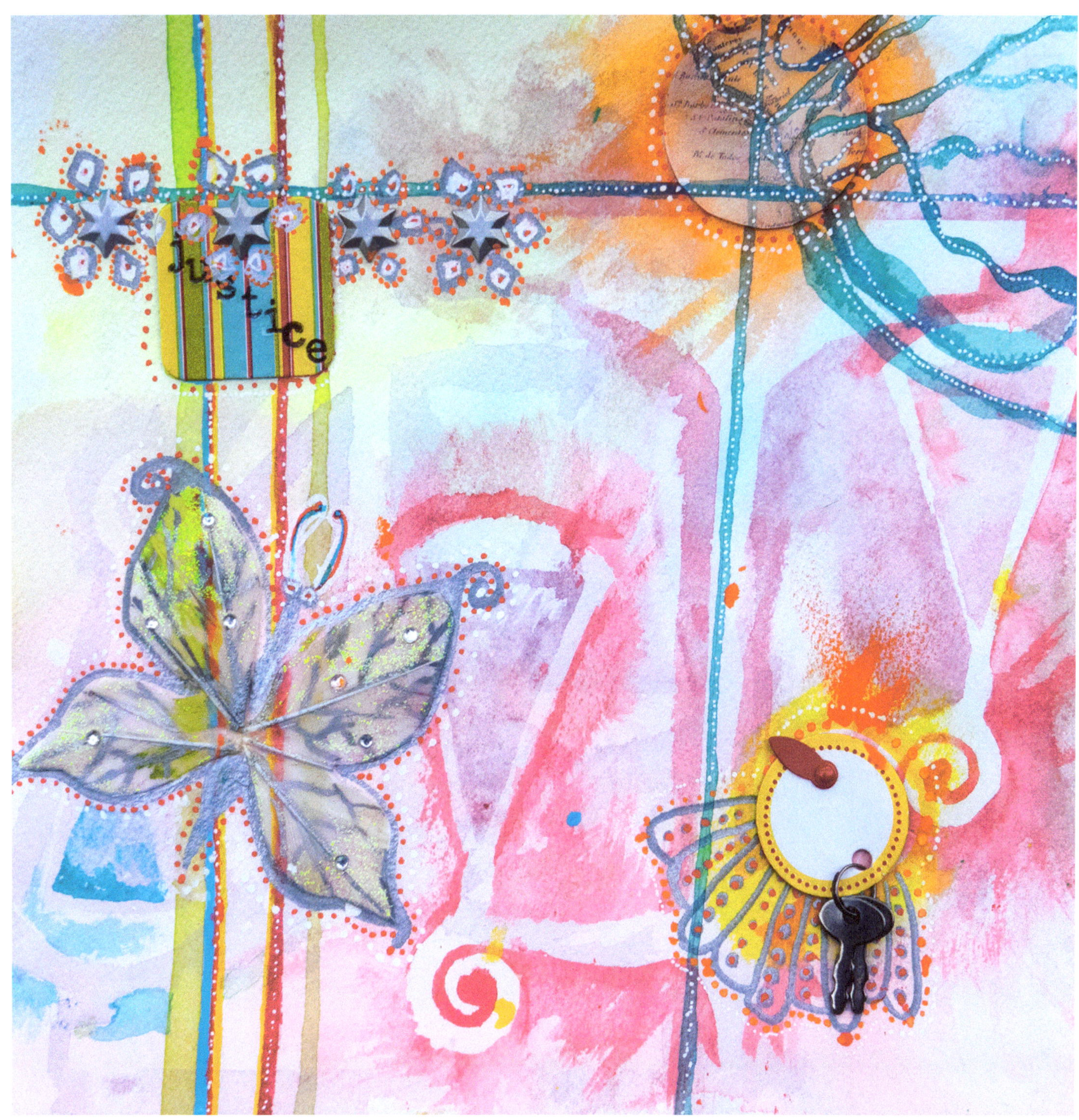
justice

Psalm 85 (NSRV)

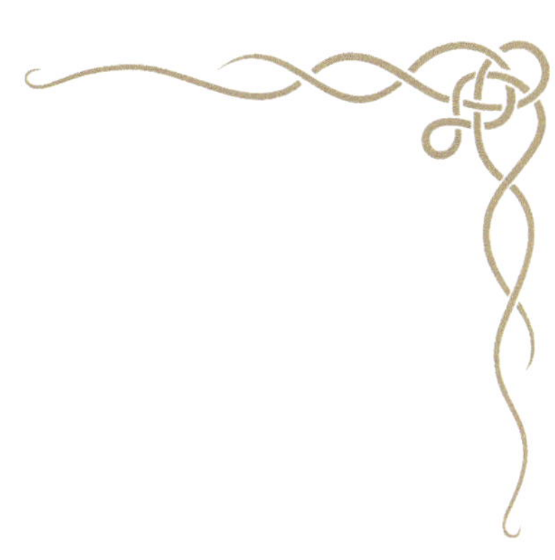

1 LORD, you were favorable to your land;
  you restored the fortunes of Jacob.
2 You forgave the iniquity of your people;
  you pardoned all their sin. Selah
3 You withdrew all your wrath;
  you turned from your hot anger.
4 Restore us again, O God of our salvation,
  and put away your indignation toward us.
5 Will you be angry with us forever?
Will you prolong your anger to all generations?
6 Will you not revive us again,
  so that your people may rejoice in you?
7 Show us your steadfast love, O LORD,
  and grant us your salvation.
8 Let me hear what God the LORD will speak,
  for he will speak peace to his people,
to his faithful, to those who turn to him in their hearts.
9 Surely his salvation is at hand for those who fear him,
  that his glory may dwell in our land.
10 Steadfast love and faithfulness will meet;
  righteousness and peace will kiss each other.
11 Faithfulness will spring up from the ground,
  and righteousness will look down from the sky.
12 The LORD will give what is good,
  and our land will yield its increase.
13 Righteousness will go before him,
  and will make a path for his steps.

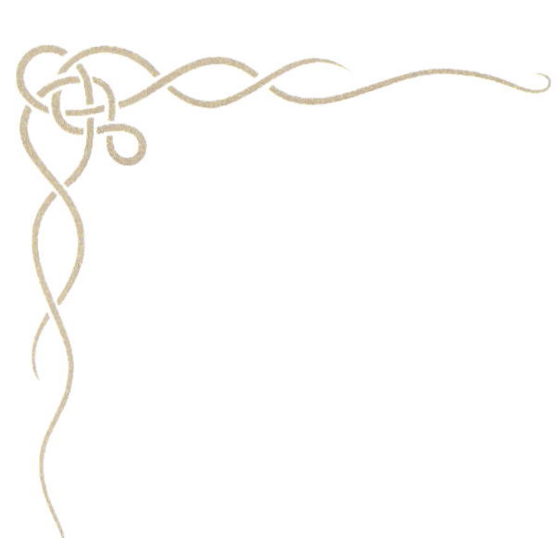

The humble realizations of one's mistakes are evident in this psalm. The writer speaks to God, reminding of times of forgiveness in the past, mindful that this is what is needed now. Will God listen? Will God forgive people's wrong-doings? And then, this line: "Steadfast love and faithfulness will meet; righteousness and peace will kiss each other." That steadfast love, God's greatest gift to humanity, is incredible in and of itself, but combined with the faith of the people, becomes something else entirely. It is a messy, dramatic, beautiful, and often taken for granted phenomenon that can only happen when God's people accept God's love, and believe that love's power is stronger than their own.

Rev. Erin Beardemphl

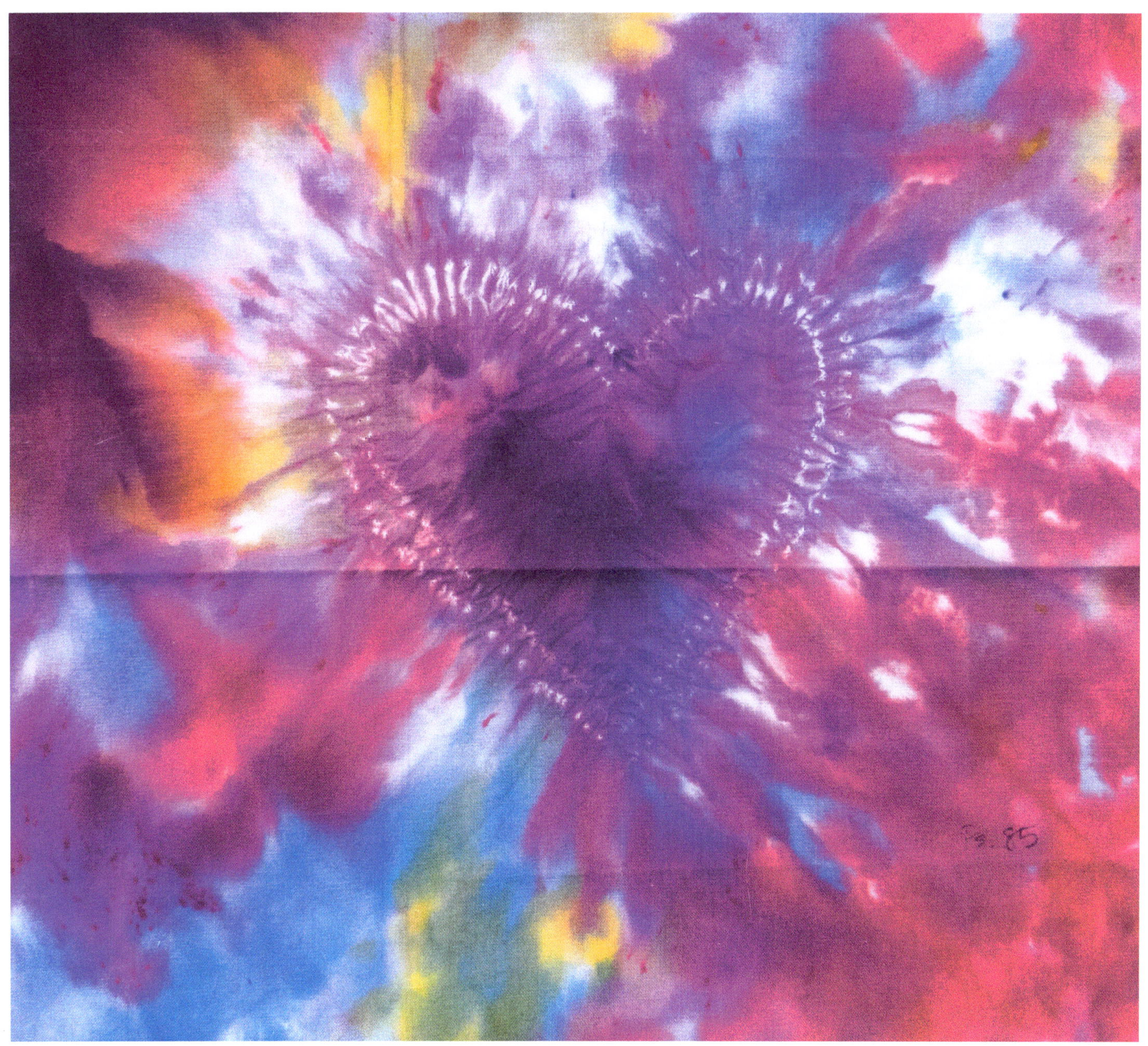
78.85

Psalm 91 (MSG)

1-13 You who sit down in the High God's presence,
spend the night in Shaddai's shadow,
Say this: "GOD, you're my refuge.
I trust in you and I'm safe!"
That's right—he rescues you from hidden traps,
shields you from deadly hazards.
His huge outstretched arms protect you—
under them you're perfectly safe;
his arms fend off all harm.
Fear nothing—not wild wolves in the night,
not flying arrows in the day,
Not disease that prowls through the darkness,
not disaster that erupts at high noon.
Even though others succumb all around,
drop like flies right and left,
no harm will even graze you.
You'll stand untouched, watch it all from a distance,
watch the wicked turn into corpses.
Yes, because GOD's your refuge,
the High God your very own home,
Evil can't get close to you,
harm can't get through the door.
He ordered his angels
to guard you wherever you go.
If you stumble, they'll catch you;
their job is to keep you from falling.
You'll walk unharmed among lions and snakes,
and kick young lions and serpents from the path.

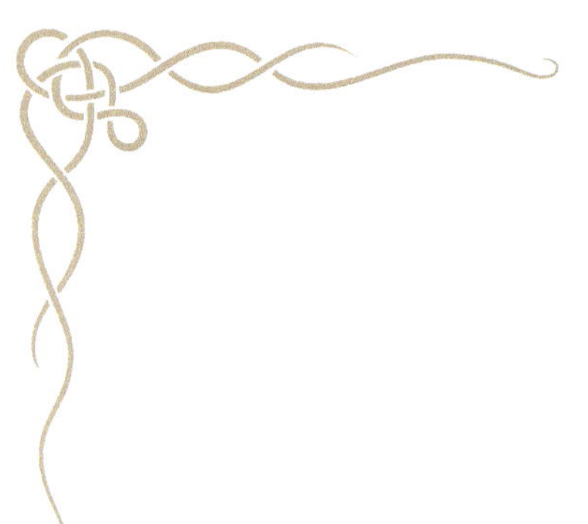

14-16 "If you'll hold on to me for dear life," says GOD,
"I'll get you out of any trouble.
I'll give you the best of care
if you'll only get to know and trust me.
Call me and I'll answer, be at your side in bad times;
I'll rescue you, then throw you a party.
I'll give you a long life,
give you a long drink of salvation!"

Psalm 91 was inscribed into a bridge where I was hiking and contemplating this Psalter project. It feels like it chose me. "His huge outstretched arms protect you, under them you are perfectly safe; his arms fend off all harm." The large image of a right hand symbolizes the size of those protective arms and threat to the creature below. "He ordered his angels to guard you wherever you go." The eagle appears throughout the Bible as a symbol of strength and protection. A soaring bald eagle expresses my belief that all winged creatures are angels on earth.

Jessica Lea

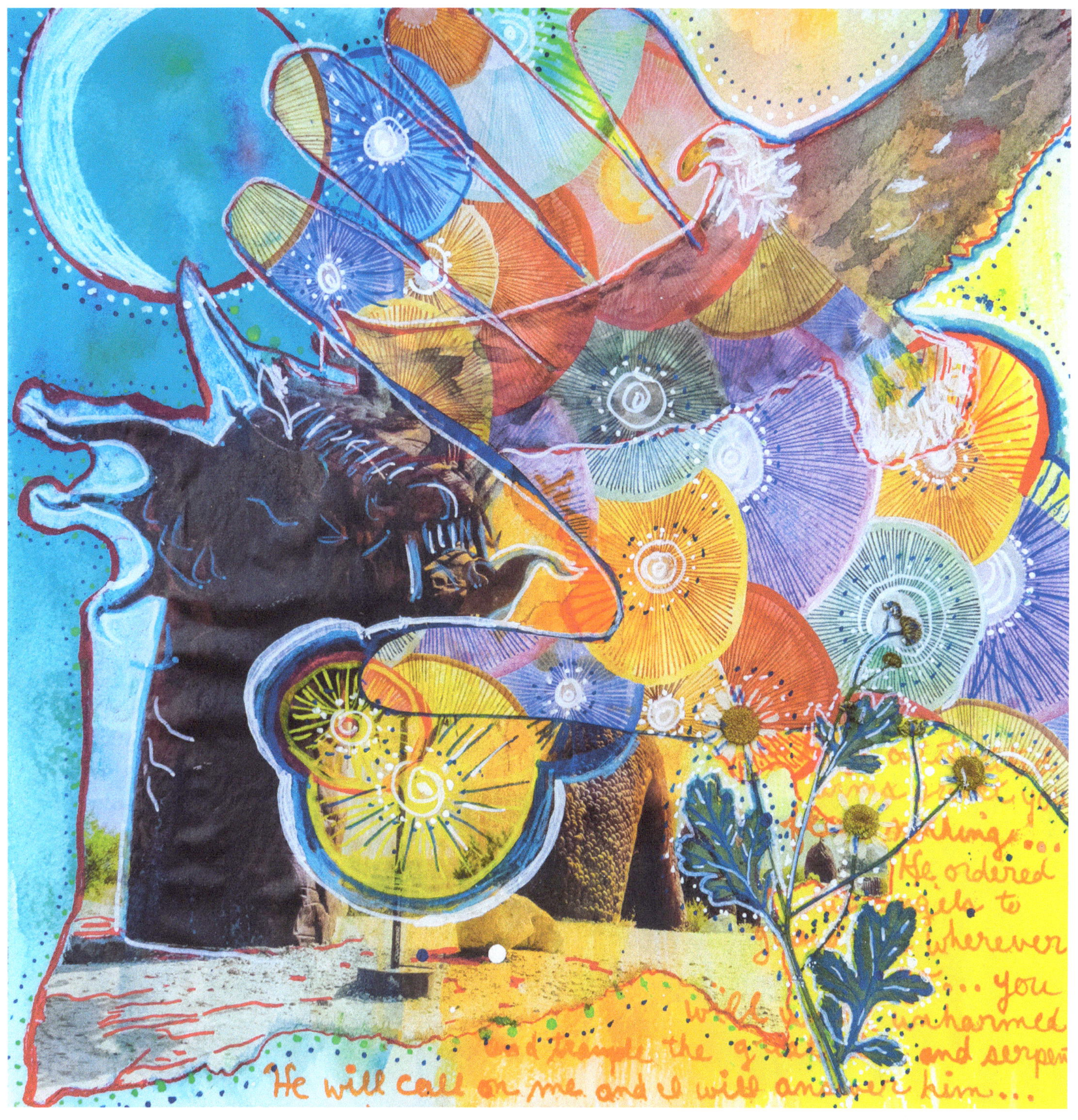
He ordered
...els to
...wherever
...you
...unharmed
...and serpe...
He will call on me and I will answer him...

Psalm 100 (NSRV)

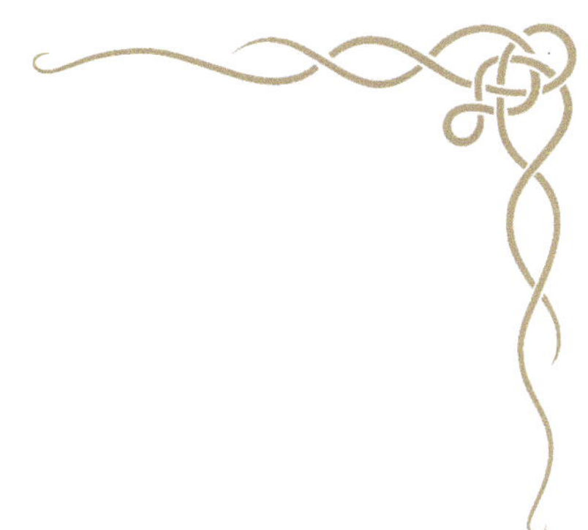

1 Make a joyful noise to the LORD, all the earth.
2   Worship the LORD with gladness;
      come into his presence with singing.
3 Know that the LORD is God.
It is he that made us, and we are his;
we are his people, and the sheep of his pasture.
4 Enter his gates with thanksgiving,
      and his courts with praise.
Give thanks to him, bless his name.
5 For the LORD is good;
his steadfast love endures forever,
and his faithfulness to all generations.

How does one show a "joyful noise to the Lord"? What exactly does praise look like? While I considered this short, bright psalm, colors sprang into my mind in splashes and streaks. When we want to celebrate, we add color to our surroundings; whether it be in posters, with streamers, pinatas, or table dressings, we use color to set the tone. My joyful noise is a cacophony of hues, carefully lain, and appearing rampant, an exuberant backdrop for the "sheep of God's pasture." Each of us creates a "joyful noise" in our own way, praising God with our individual talents as we are able. All of it is heard and experienced by the One who created and is creating. I like to think that our cacophonous rainbow is pleasing indeed.

Rev. Erin Beardemphl

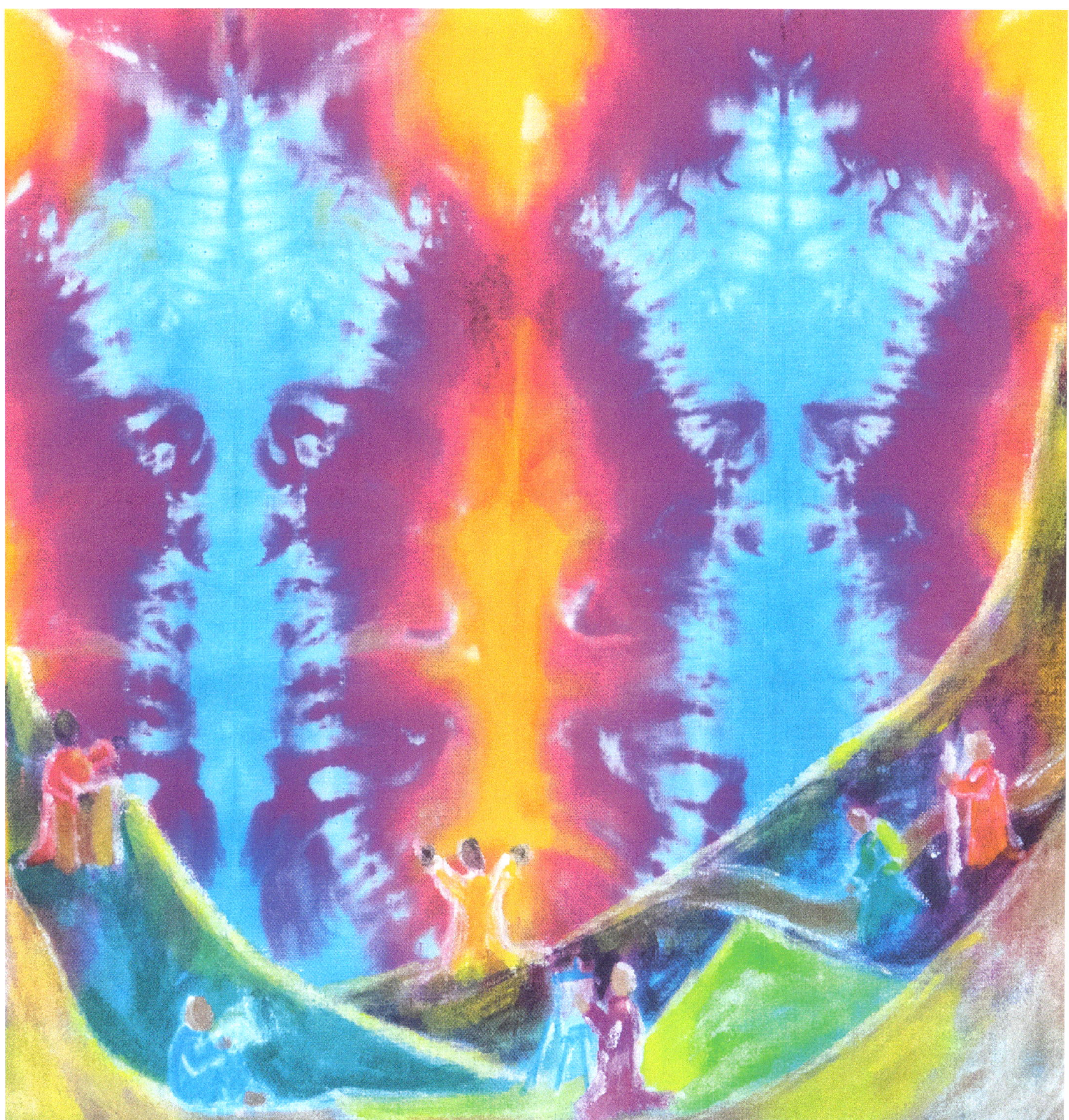

Psalm 126 (NSRV)

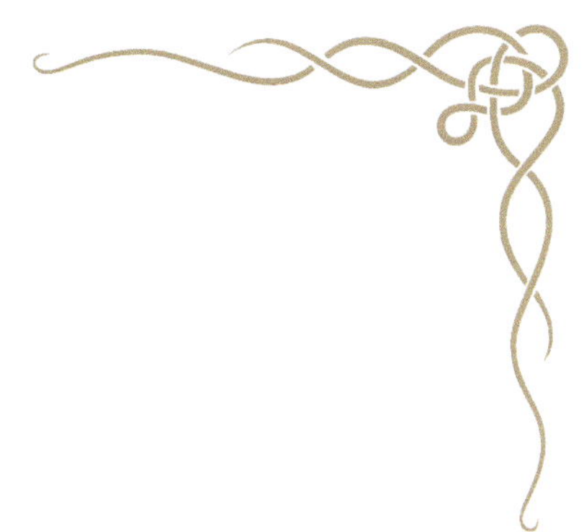

1 When the LORD restored the fortunes of Zion,
we were like those who dream.
2 Then our mouth was filled with laughter,
and our tongue with shouts of joy;
then it was said among the nations,
"The LORD has done great things for them."
3 The LORD has done great things for us,
and we rejoiced.
4 Restore our fortunes, O LORD,
like the watercourses in the Negeb.
5 May those who sow in tears
reap with shouts of joy.
6 Those who go out weeping,
bearing the seed for sowing,
shall come home with shouts of joy,
carrying their sheaves.

"When the Lord restored the fortunes of Zion, we were like those who dream." Is it real? Can our suffering be over? Will we really be able to work again? Feed ourselves again? Live again without fear? The very idea that this could be a possibility is cause in itself for celebration. It is also what prompts the psalmist to call out to God for restoration. The land is sown with tears, but it is faith in God's redeeming nature and stead-fast love which leads to the harvest of joy. There is work in sowing seed, and care in growing the plants. It is not simply believing that God will save a people, but working alongside what you know of God, that leads to covenants between Creator and Created, harvests of joy walking as though in a dream.

Rev. Erin Beardemphl

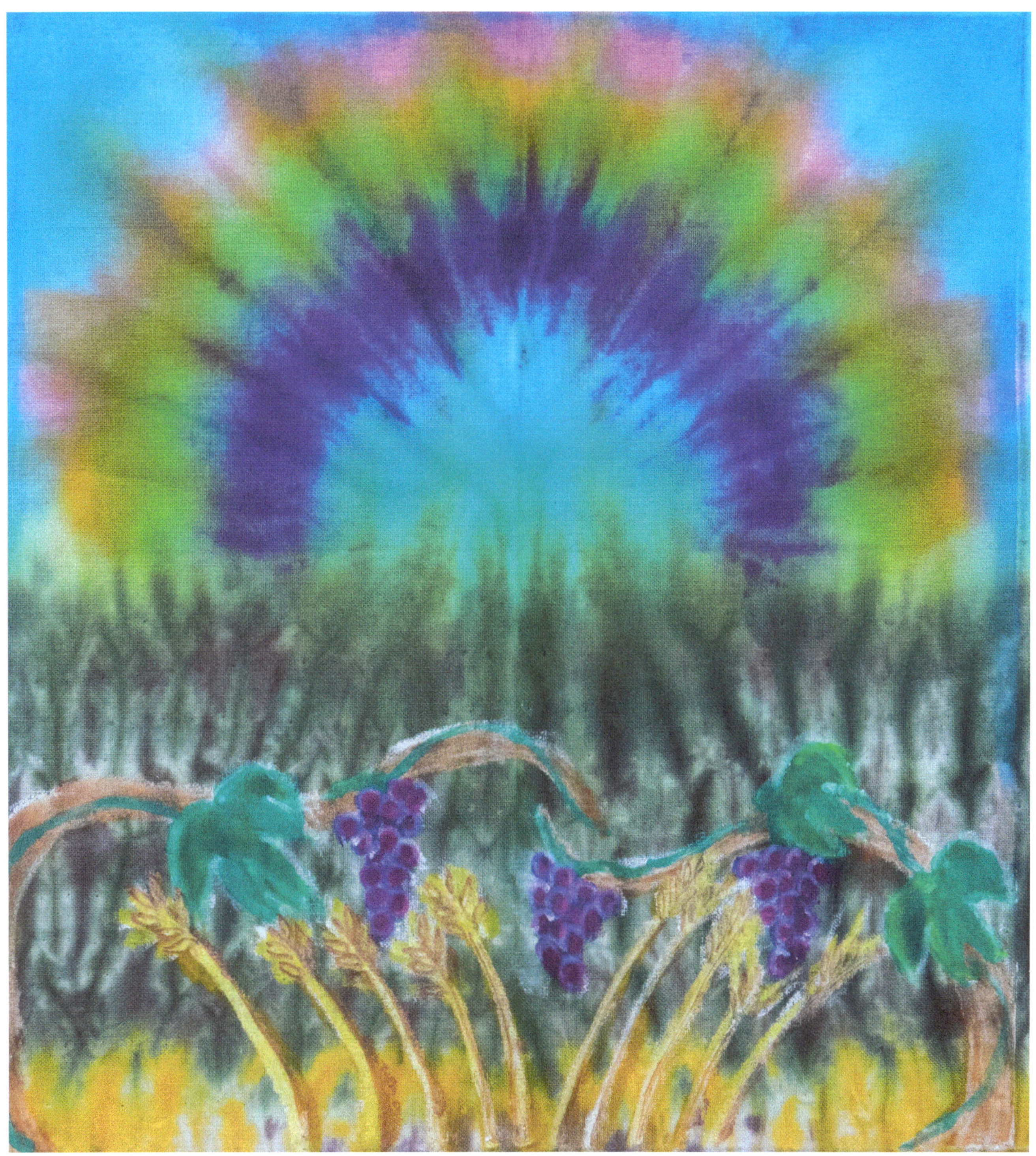

Psalm 139 (NSRV)

1 O LORD, you have searched me and known me.
2 You know when I sit down and when I rise up;
        you discern my thoughts from far away.
3 You search out my path and my lying down,
        and are acquainted with all my ways.
4 Even before a word is on my tongue,
    O LORD, you know it completely.
5 You hem me in, behind and before,
        and lay your hand upon me.
6 Such knowledge is too wonderful for me;
        it is so high that I cannot attain it.
7 Where can I go from your spirit?
    Or where can I flee from your presence?
8 If I ascend to heaven, you are there;
    if I make my bed in Sheol, you are there.
9 If I take the wings of the morning
    and settle at the farthest limits of the sea,
10 even there your hand shall lead me,
    and your right hand shall hold me fast.
11 If I say, "Surely the darkness shall cover me,
        and the light around me become night,"
12 even the darkness is not dark to you;
        the night is as bright as the day,
        for darkness is as light to you.
13 For it was you who formed my inward parts;
    you knit me together in my mother's womb.
14 I praise you, for I am fearfully and wonderfully made.
    Wonderful are your works;
        that I know very well.

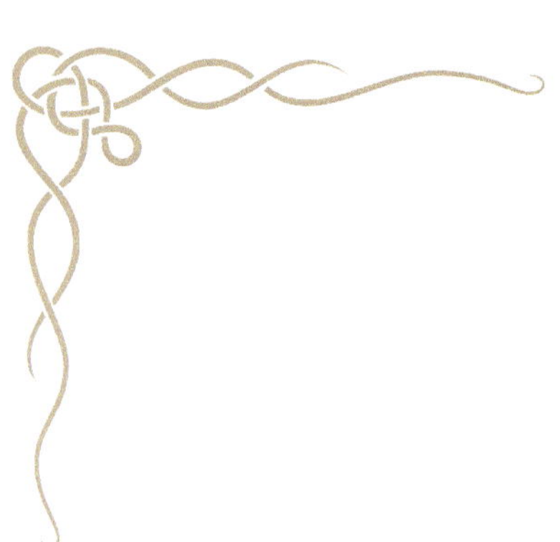

15   My frame was not hidden from you,
        when I was being made in secret,
    intricately woven in the depths of the earth.
16 Your eyes beheld my unformed substance.
        In your book were written
      all the days that were formed for me,
        when none of them as yet existed.
17 How weighty to me are your thoughts, O God!
        How vast is the sum of them!
18 I try to count them—they are more than the sand;
      I come to the end—I am still with you.
19 O that you would kill the wicked, O God,
    and that the bloodthirsty would depart from me—
      20 those who speak of you maliciously,
      and lift themselves up against you for evil!
21 Do I not hate those who hate you, O LORD?
    And do I not loathe those who rise up against you?
      22 I hate them with perfect hatred;
          I count them my enemies.
23 Search me, O God, and know my heart;
        test me and know my thoughts.
24 See if there is any wicked way in me,
      and lead me in the way everlasting.

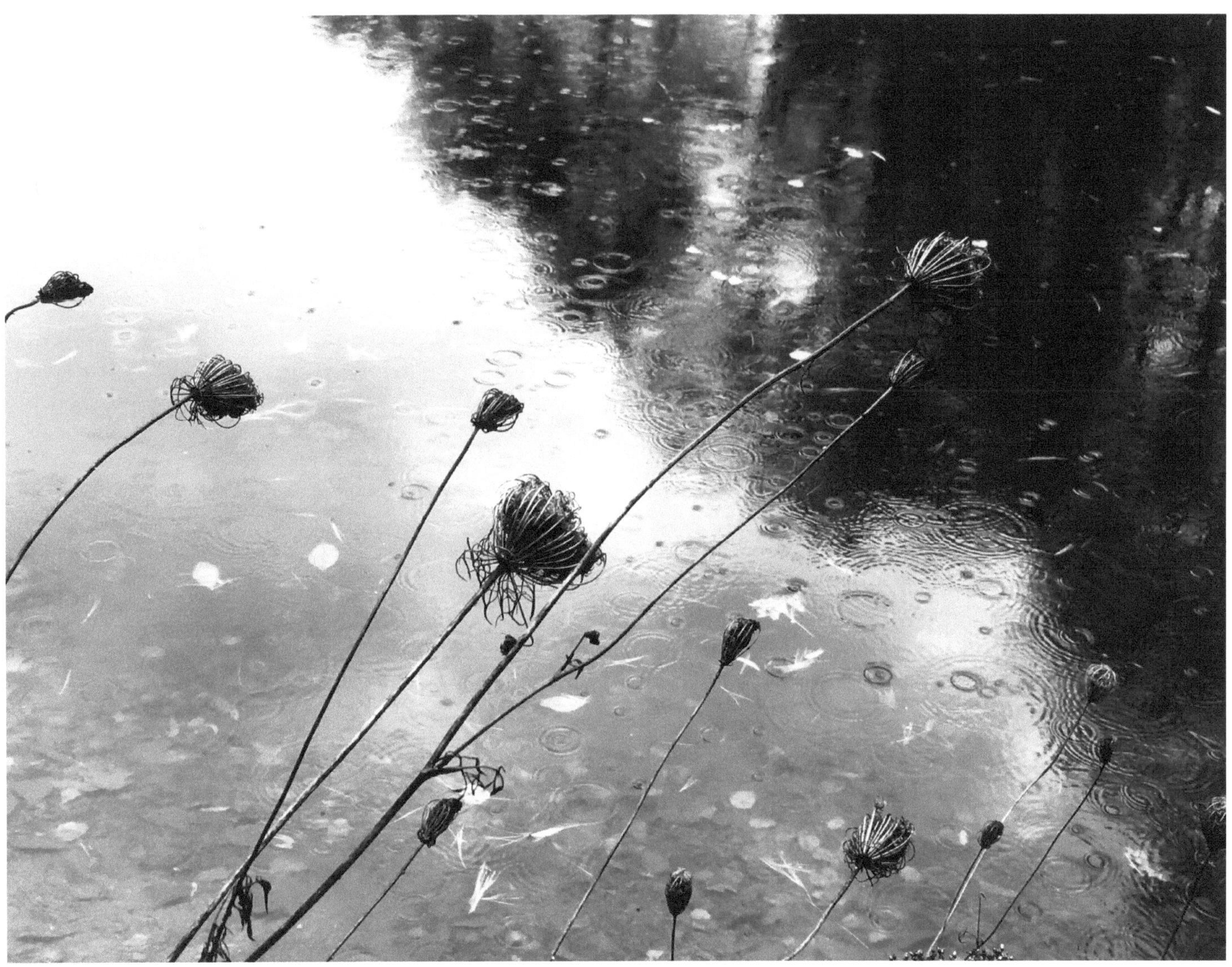

I have loved the psalms since I was a young girl growing up in Colorado. I have also loved the natural world and felt surrounded and immersed in the wonder and beauty of the seasons. The Rocky Mountains were always there to hold and protect me. That's how I saw it. As a young mom, I found tranquility sitting on the floor in my kitchen late at night, when my kids were asleep, with a Bible and my guitar, making up melodies to favorite psalms. I also discovered the Chinese art of Brush Painting a few years ago, being entranced by the idea of becoming "one with the brush" and finding in this artistic approach a kinship with my search for the "Essence of Life." So, when the opportunity to pick a psalm, illustrate it, and reflect on it in writing presented itself, I was excited! I got my brushes, ink and rice paper out and began practicing brush strokes in anticipation of illustrating Psalm 139, a very favorite psalm. This psalm, the natural world, and my history of seeking the Divine through Christianity, Buddhist and Taoist philosophy (did you know that the word for "nature" in Chinese comes from Taoism and means "things as they are"?) and Native American "Life Ways" was calling to me! The Essence of Life was calling to me.

Except Brush Painting is a tremendous discipline and takes a lifetime to master. I thought I could get far enough to do a very simple illustration. It was not to be. I plan to continue my Brush Painting practice, but have chosen a photograph I did a couple years ago for my illustration. The psalm and this photograph of nature speak to me of essence, the Great Mystery we are in that suffuses every single thing in this world, human and "more than human." It is Love. "Where can I go then from your Spirit? Where can I flee from your presence?" The Inescapable Love of the Divine, whatever Name we give the Unnamable, traces our journeys, is familiar with all our ways, holds everything in this world in an embrace, and does not let go.

Sue Hammond

Psalm 150 (NSRV)

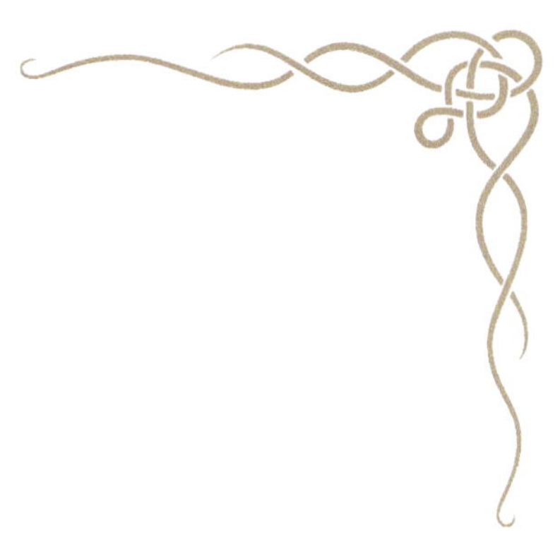

1 Praise the LORD!
Praise God in his sanctuary;
praise him in his mighty firmament!
2 Praise him for his mighty deeds;
praise him according to his surpassing greatness!
3 Praise him with trumpet sound;
praise him with lute and harp!
4 Praise him with tambourine and dance;
praise him with strings and pipe!
5 Praise him with clanging cymbals;
praise him with loud clashing cymbals!
6 Let everything that breathes praise the LORD!
Praise the LORD!

God's holy house of worship is the entire world. Everything outside, under the open skies is his work of art, his magnificent acts of greatness, his palette. One can only believe that all was created by a higher power while watching the first light of the morning, as it grows brighter and brighter from the heavens, to become a golden fiery brilliance onto the lands. As the light shines, the colors of the mountains and the trees grow more vibrant by the second and are amplified by the reflections from the calm waters below.

I hear an orchestra, a symphony of divine music in the back of my mind. Growing louder and louder as the heavens light up a new day. Being witness to something so magical is an experience like no other.

Drew Morgan

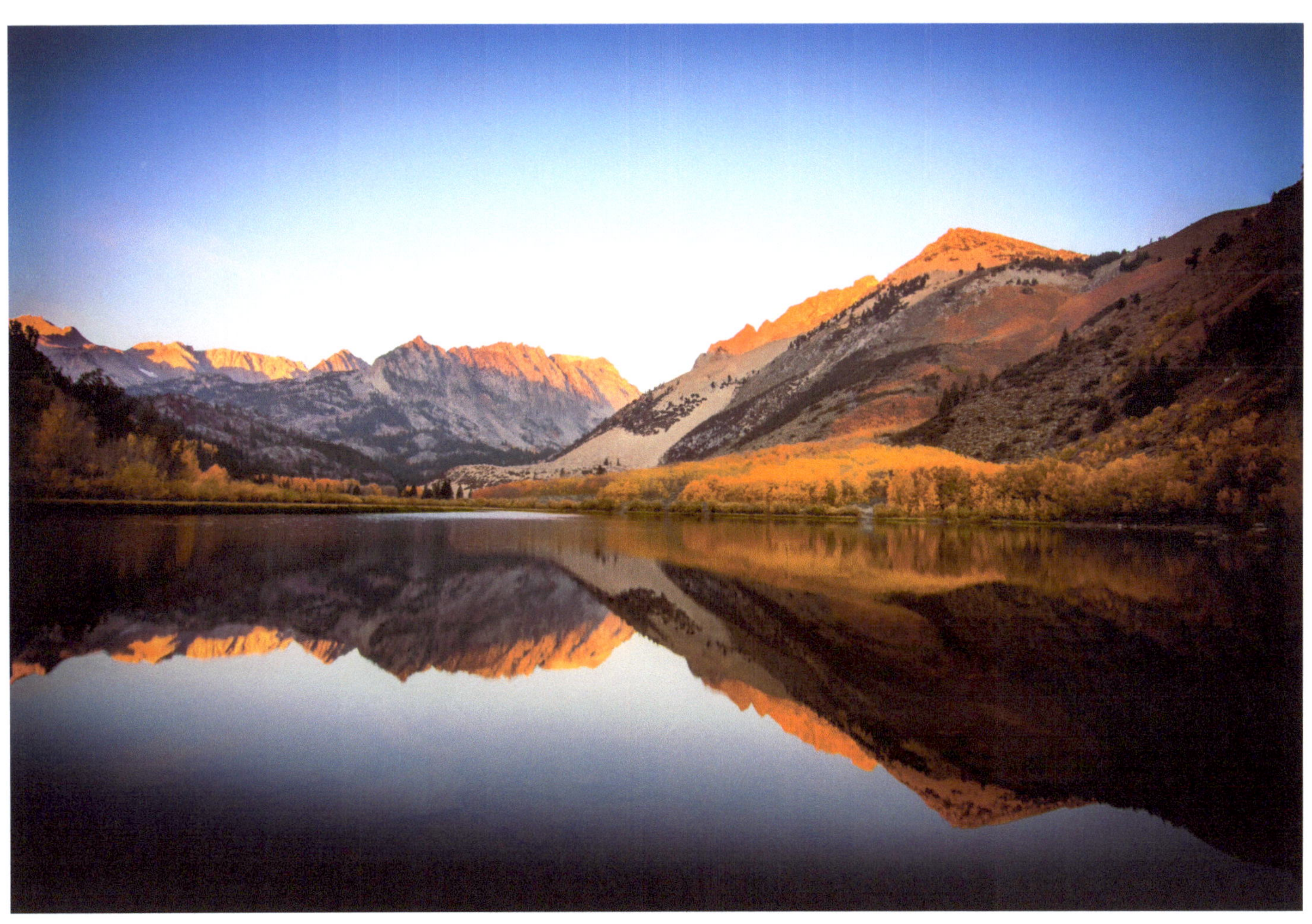

Biographies

Rev. Erin GH Beardemphl

Rev. Erin GH Beardemphl is a liturgical artist and Honorary Minister for Arts and Worship at Redlands United Church of Christ. She is a regular contributor to the Living Psalms Project of the United Church of Christ, and was a featured artist of the "52 Project" at the Riverside Art Museum in 2019. Her ministries change and evolve over time, but her first love is teaching others how to find their own spirituality in artistic and creative experiments.

Sue Hammond

Susan Hammond is a grateful woman, mother of four daughters, grandmother of eight grandchildren. She loves the natural world, walking Lulu the dog, playing guitar, singing, and reading profusely. She draws knowledge from the trees, the birds, the children and the rivers.

Jessica Lea

Artist at heart and lawyer by trade, Jessica Lea is a New York transplant living in the Inland Empire. She was a featured artist in the 52 Project 2019 and 2021 Exhibitions at Riverside Art Museum and is a member of the Inlandia Institute. In 2020, Jessica published Diamonds and Yoga Pants, her first book of poems. Jessica is currently working on an ekphrastic collection of haiku, multimedia visual journaling, and learning how to use her Canon Rebel camera by taking pictures of trees and birds.

Mary Melcher

Mary Leona Melcher is a retired public high school art and other subjects teacher. Her many years at a continuation high school gave her the opportunity to uncover and support her students' creativity, and she feels blessed by a career she loved. She remembers standing in front of cave paintings in France, feeling connected and going back in time to those original "mark makers." She paints with this in mind and continues to encourage creative activity in others.

Drew Morgan

In between working as a paralegal and spending time with his family, Drew Morgan hits the road with his camera when he can in search of adventure. As of late, Drew's passion has been night photography, capturing the Milky Way and the starry heavens.

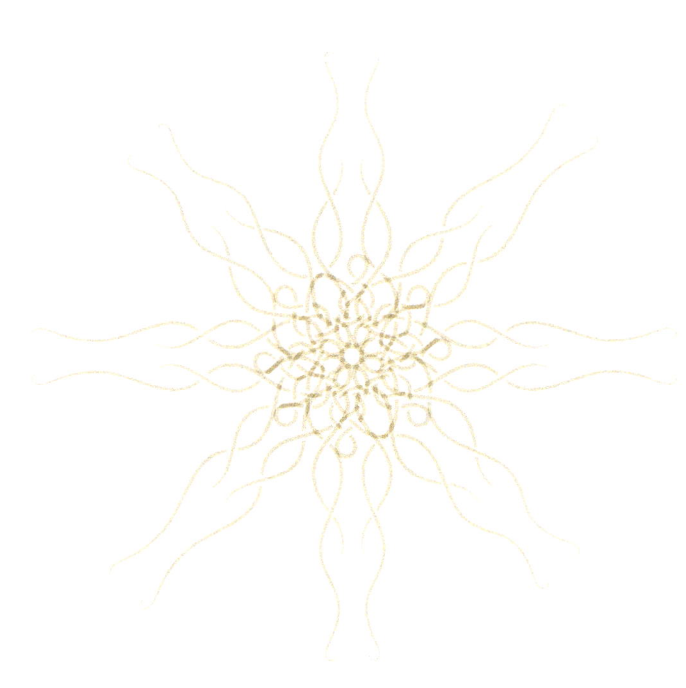

Cindy Rinne

Cindy Rinne is a San Bernardino artist and poet who has created fine art for over 40 years. She started creating fiber art over 30 years ago. She has participated in several online group exhibitions through LAAA/825. Cindy has exhibited tapestries in "Woven Stories" at MOAH (Lancaster Museum of Art and History) and at RAFFMA at Cal State San Bernardino for "Voices of Ancient Palmyra Resounded." She participated in "50/50, FIFTY/FIFTY, The Creative Magic of Collaboration" at the Progress Gallery in Pomona, CA in 2017. In 2020, Cindy was selected for "Hobson's Choice" at the Torrance Art Museum. She has also exhibited at the Beatnik Lounge JTAG, and La Matadora Gallery in Joshua Tree and is represented by Desert Peach Gallery in Yucca Valley, CA.

Larry Rose

Trained as a photographer at the Art Center College of Design, Larry Rose has worked as a photojournalist for newspapers and magazines, as well as commercial and advertising projects. In addition, he taught photography at the college and university levels. Now, he is enjoying retirement and capturing images for himself and to share with others.